The Coming American Dictatorship

John Silveira

ISBN 978-0-9821577-5-6
Copyright 2000-2009

Backwoods Home Magazine
PO Box 712
Gold Beach, Oregon 97444
www.backwoodshome.com

Edited by Ilene Duffy
Cover design by Annie Tuttle

Contents

Introduction

Far from being the "land of the free," the United States of America is now the most regulated society in history, with laws covering every aspect of our existence. The assaults on our freedoms come from within, namely, from our own government, including our Presidents, Congress, courts, and bureaucracy. They come from the left and the right, from both Democratic and Republican parties, and include:

- replacing our individual rights with collective rights
- subverting the jury process
- reinterpreting the *Constitution*
- creating phony emergencies
- creating a vast bureaucracy that lies beyond the reach of both the voters and the Congress
- increasing the power of the Presidency with Executive Orders

The U.S. also has more people in prison, jail, or in the probation system, in both absolute numbers and as a percentage of our population, than any other country. This is even when we include current or former communist countries, Moslem countries, and the third world dictatorships of Asia, Africa, and South America. We may have only 5% of the world's population, but we have 25% of the world's prison population.

This anthology of articles not only describes the problem, but explains what we, as freedom-loving Americans, can do about it.

— John Silveira

Part I

How the erosion of our natural rights is destroying our freedom

Yesterday a voice asked, "Hey, Silveira!" I looked up. It was Dave Duffy, the publisher of *Backwoods Home Magazine*. He was fingering through his Rolodex. Without looking at me he asked, "Have you got Mac's number?" I knew he meant O.E. MacDougal, his poker-playing friend from southern California.

We had just gone through deadline and it had been frantic for weeks here on the editorial side of the magazine. Now there was a calm, the kind thunderstorms leave behind.

"I've got it on my computer," I said and started to open my address file.

"Forget it," he said. He was holding one of the Rolodex cards in his hand and he picked up his phone and started to punch in a number.

My address file was open by now. I closed it.

"What's up?" I asked.

"I want to see if he wants to come up. Maybe we can get him up here after deadline."

"Deadline's over," I said.

"Yeah," he said.

"Sounds good to me," I said and I turned back to my computer, but I listened as he left an invitation on Mac's answering machine. He told him he should come up, go fishing, kick back, drink beer—all the usual things.

When he hung up, he asked, "When's the last time he was up here?"

I thought about it. "Last fall, I think."

Like I said, that was yesterday. So, this morning, you can imagine my surprise when we got into the office and there was Mac asleep under the table that holds the printer. Dave had left his message barely 18 hours earlier and Mac lives 800 miles south of us. But there he was, under a blanket, on the floor.

Dave came in right behind me and stopped.

Mac opened one eye and looked at us.

"Are you okay?" Dave asked.

"Sure," Mac said and he got up from the floor like an old bull stretching his muscles.

"What are you doing on the floor? Why didn't you come up to my house or stay at one of the motels in town?"

"I got in around 2 a.m. and I'd had some brainstorms while I was driving. I wanted to do some stuff on your computer before I slept. When I finished...well..." He pointed to the floor.

"How'd you get in? Did I give you a key?" Dave asked.

"No."

"Well, how...?"

Mac looked at Dave.

"Oh," Dave said and turned on his computer.

Something was left unsaid about the way Mac got in.

"What have you been doing the last few months?" Dave asked.

"Playing poker."

"How's Carol?"

Carol was his girlfriend. I'd met her a few times when I used to live down in southern California.

Mac didn't answer.

"How's she doing?" Dave asked again.

"I haven't seen her in a few months."

"Oh," Dave responded. After a slight pause he asked, "Any new prospects on the horizon?"

"None yet...I've seen your 'End of the World' specials," Mac said. He was changing the subject. "They're pretty creative."

"Yeah, they're fun to do," Dave said as he put his stuff down and sat down at his computer. It was going through the opening screens.

"I haven't seen you in almost a year," I said to Mac. "Did you survive Y2K okay?"

He smiled. "Yeah, talk about a bust. I never thought it would amount to much, but I didn't expect it to be a nothing."

"How's the world going to end next time?" Dave asked.

Mac gave him a quizzical look.

"You know," Dave added, "what do you think's going to be the next big problem that will *end civilization as we know it*?"

"Real or imagined problems?" Mac asked.

"That sounds like a trick question."

"There's no trick," Mac said. "It's just that some scenarios are imaginary, like the ones you see on the covers of the tabloids in the checkout line at the grocery market. But there are others that are credible and should be of concern."

"Okay," Dave said. "So let's make it real." He clicked on a screen icon and his computer started dialing up our Internet service provider.

"The coming American dictatorship," Mac replied.

Dave glanced back for a moment, then looked back at his monitor. "Is there a punch line to this?" he asked.

"I hadn't planned on one."

"Come on, do you actually think a dictatorship is possible in this country?" I asked.

"A dictatorship is possible anywhere. Throughout history dictatorships are the conditions under which most people have lived."

Neither Dave nor I said anything but I could tell Dave was losing interest in downloading his e-mail.

"Pick any time in history," Mac continued. "Then make a mental estimate of what percentage of humanity lived under dictatorships of one kind or another at that time. There have even been times when everyone on the planet lived under a dictatorship of one sort or another."

There was another brief silence as neither Dave nor I responded.

"And, as if we can't stand freedom, it seems as if every place men *have* won freedoms, the generations that followed them gave them away. Always. There's evidence that that's what we're doing now."

"Now?" I asked.

"Yes."

"Us? We're doing it...in the United States?"

"That seems to be the way the wind is blowing."

"We have a *Constitution* that won't let that happen" I said.

"The *Constitution* will still be there and not a word of it will be changed nor will it have been amended. It will remain in place, a showcase to the world, but it will mean nothing."

"What's happening that makes you feel that way?" Dave asked.

"We're putting all the mechanisms in place that will make one possible. Two hundred years ago, our Founding Fathers had put as many obstacles as possible in the way of a dictatorship because they feared that unless there were obstacles, specifically, the safeguards in our *Constitution*, a dictatorship was inevitable.

"But even then, many of them weren't optimistic about our chances. When Benjamin Franklin was leaving the Constitutional Convention, a Mrs. Powell of Philadelphia asked, 'Well, Doctor, what have we got, a republic or a monarchy?' Franklin replied, 'A republic if you can keep it.' He expressed the sentiment of many of the delegates.

"Today, as if we're bent on proving the cynicism in Franklin's reply was deserved, we're ignoring—no, we're actually throwing away—the safeguards hammered out among the delegates to that Convention.

We're not changing the wording or the intent of the *Constitution*, we're just ignoring it."

"What's happening that makes you see a dictatorship coming?" Dave asked.

Mac put his hands behind his head and leaned back in his chair. He was thinking. "If I had to summarize what's happening," he said, "I'd have to say there's not just one thing we have to worry about; there's a whole bunch of things that are undermining our freedoms. But I'm not going to say there's a conspiracy, like some people do, though there may be. I really don't know. But I'd have to say that if there's a concerted attack on our liberties, whoever's doing it is a lot smarter than we are and he—or they—have my grudging admiration because these changes aren't being forced on us, we're just going along with them."

"So, give us some examples of what's making a dictatorship imminent," I said.

Six signs of the end of America's freedoms

Mac thought again. "There are six things that I'd say are sure signs that we're in trouble.

"First there's the steady erosion of our basic rights, the ones a lot of people call our constitutional rights, though that's not a good name for them. It's better to think of them as natural rights, the way our Founding Fathers did—or think of them as God-given rights if you want. Thinking of them as constitutional rights is part of what is getting us in trouble. You have to realize that our Founding Fathers didn't think of them as constitutional rights because they knew that if our rights are provided by either the *Constitution* or the government, what the government gives, it can also take away. As natural or God-given rights, they're absolute. That's the way they were intended.

"The next problem we have is related to this erosion of our rights, but I'd treat it as a whole separate category. It's the unintended consequences of having created new rights—legal rights created by Congress and which Congress and bureaucrats have decided supercede or nullify our natural rights. These include the new rights that have come about as a result of the *Civil Rights Act of 1964*, the *Environmental Protection Act*, and the American Disabilities Act. Unlike our natural rights, which come to us at the expense of no one else, the new rights *have to be* provided by someone else. It's in *having* to provide them that our government has found ways to erode our natural rights.

"Third there's the unconstitutional bypassing of our legislative process by the President—not just this one in office now, but by all of the recent presidents.

"Using what are called *Executive Orders*, they create laws that are not only illegal and unconstitutional, but are created without the consent of the Congress or the people of the United States. Some of these edicts, believe it or not, explicitly suspend the *Constitution* for an indeterminate amount of time on the whim of the President.

"Fourth, there's the new rules and regulations imposed on businesses by our federal government by which the government circumvents our Fifth Amendment rights by insisting businesses spy on us. This includes banks, airlines, and even manufacturers of things like light bulbs and paper.

> *With respect to the words general welfare, I have always regarded them as qualified by the detail of powers (enumerated in the Constitution) connected with them. To take them in a literal and unlimited sense would be a metamorphosis of the Constitution into a character which there is a host of proofs was not contemplated by its creators.*
>
> **James Madison**
> **1751-1836**
> **4th President**
> **of the United States**
> **"Father" of the Constitution**

"Fifth is the creation of a professional, standing army. The Founding Fathers feared a professional army. They believed this country should depend on the militia—and I'm using the word 'militia' in the way they used it in the *Second Amendment*, meaning the body of citizen, not the National Guard or some other professional organization. Professional armies lose their allegiance to the citizenry and have a history of becoming the accomplices of tyrants. It's highly unlikely there would have been any protests to the illegal war we fought in Vietnam if we'd had a professional army then.

"Last of all, but not least, our economy is no longer a true free market economy. It is now one of the socialist economies. We're now a fascist economy. For all of our posturing about how bad fascism is, we have created a fascist economy as a compromise between capitalism and communism.

"All of these changes are milestones on the road to tyranny. If they had all been invoked at once, we'd have seen them for what they are, an attempt to subvert what had once been the freest society history has ever seen. There'd have been a revolution in this country; blood would have run in the streets. But they've come over generations, and the American people, whose collective attention span is brief and whose memory is even shorter, have come to believe that the way things are in this country today is the way they've always been."

"It sounds like you're saying you believe we will definitely have a dictatorship," Dave said.

"I'd like to be able to say we won't, but I believe we will. I don't know when, and I'll admit I could even be proved wrong. Maybe, even though we are putting all mechanisms for a dictatorship into place...maybe it won't happen. Though why we'd want to tempt fate by putting all the machinery for a dictatorship in place, I don't know. But if I had to bet, I'd say that sometime in the not too distant future we will live under tyranny. Sometime after that historians are going to look back to where the United States stood on the dawn of the new millennium and wonder if we'd gone mad or if we were just idiots. History is not going to treat us well; I can almost assure you of that."

"What do you mean we have a fascist economy?" I asked.

"Wait a minute, let's take these in order," Dave said. He was now sitting back in his chair and had his feet up on the desk that is usually behind him. He had a yellow legal pad on one knee and a pencil in his hand. He was taking notes. "You said there are..." on his legal pad he counted the points Mac had made. "...six things that are bringing on a dictatorship. The first, you said, is the erosion of our rights."

"You should get off line," Mac said to Dave as he pointed to the computer behind him.

"Oh, yeah," Dave said, and he closed his Net connection.

Losing our natural rights

When Dave turned back he said, "Okay, start at the beginning—losing our rights. First of all, who's to blame for all of this?"

"The politicians and the bureaucrats," I said.

Mac seemed to consider what I'd said.

"Is that who you'd blame?" Dave asked Mac.

Mac looked up at the ceiling again. I could tell this wasn't going to be an easy answer. "You know," he said, "for decades we've been telling ourselves that to make government right, all we have to do is to get those guys in Washington to change their ways. But I don't feel that way anymore."

"Why not?" Dave asked.

"Because for years, while I've been talking to people about this very subject, I've been telling them our government is illegal, that it violates *Article I, Section 8*, of the *Constitution*, that it tramples all over the *Bill of Rights*. And just recently it dawned on me that in all those years not one person has ever said to me, 'Our government is legal; it complies with the *Constitution*.' Instead, they tell me, 'Things are different now.' Or, 'We have different problems now.'"

"So?" I said.

"No one's defending the actions of the government as legal, constitutional, or even right. They're saying they know our government doesn't operate within the confines of the *Constitution* anymore, but they say that's okay because our problems are different from the problems the Founding Fathers faced. Or they just say the *Constitution* is old. Even

Franklin Roosevelt said our *Constitution* was only fit for horse and buggy days and he never let it get in his way."

"What's your point?" Dave asked.

"The *Constitution's* being trampled on but *we the people* don't complain about it. We make no noise when the safeguards are breached. We don't protect our rights from the very entity our *Constitution* is meant to protect us from, our government itself. If we don't stop them, then it's our fault.

"The *Constitution* isn't there to tell us, the citizens, how to behave; it's there to set limits on government. We've got to hold them to it. For the first 150 years or so of this country, it worked pretty well. But now the government ignores the *Constitution* whenever it's convenient for them to do so. And I mean government at all levels—federal, state, and the local level."

"But it still sounds like all we've got to do is to get government to change," I said.

"But they won't," Mac said to me.

"Why not?" Dave asked.

"Because the American electorate doesn't want them to change. We expect the so-called average citizen to obey the law, even when it's absurd or unfair, but we don't want our politicians or bureaucrats to have to obey it if we figure there's a payoff for us. And every time we allow exceptions to the *Constitution*, we do it because we expect some kind of payoff. You see, the worst enemy of liberty is not the tyrant without, it's the tyrant within us all."

"I still think it's the fault of politicians," I said.

"You can't blame politicians who we can *vote* out of office for what they do. We're the only ones who can change things, but we don't vote them out."

"You're saying the problems in this country can't really be blamed on the politicians or the bureaucrats; they're really our fault," Dave said.

"That's exactly what I'm saying."

> *The condition upon which God hath given liberty to man is eternal vigilance; which condition if he break, servitude is at once the consequence of his crime and the punishment of his guilt.*
> **John Philpot Curran**
> **(1750-1817)**

"So we're bringing this tyranny down on ourselves."

"Yes."

"But the next batch we vote in will just do the same things," I said.

"Then you vote them out. These guys don't want to be one-term congressmen. How long do you think it'll be before they start acting like the hired help and not our masters?"

"I think they'll just keep doing what they're doing," I said.

"No," Dave interrupted, "Mac's right, they want to be more than one-term congressmen. Two or, at most, three elections in which they're being sent home and they'll learn to do what we want."

"The public opinion polls say people want lower taxes, less government..." Mac said.

"But in the ultimate polls, the elections themselves," Dave said, "we keep sending the people back to Congress who are giving us more government, more regulations, more taxes."

Mac nodded.

"Then we *are* bringing all of our problems down on ourselves," Dave said.

"That's the way I see it," Mac replied.

"So, what happened?" Dave asked. "Where'd we go wrong? How'd we go from a country that was free to this erosion of our rights?"

"You can start with one simple premise: we all want to be free, but we want to dictate to our neighbors. There's always something our neighbors do that we don't like and that we think there should be a law against. I'm not talking about murder or robbery where there's a victim and upon which we can get almost universal agreement that it's wrong. I'm talking about gambling, prostitution, drug use, putting additions on your house, wearing seat belts, how children are educated, etc. I think there should be a law against something you're doing or not doing and you, in turn, think someone should make a law against something I'm doing, and..."

He paused for a moment. "...there's always a politician trying to curry both of our votes. So he'll try to get the laws enacted, laws you want imposed on me and laws I want imposed on you. So we get drug laws, zoning laws, laws about politically correct speech, guns laws, restrictions on businesses—you name it and somebody wants it outlawed or regulated and there's a politician somewhere listening. But you can't blame *him*. He's just doing what both you and I and all of our neighbors are trying to do to each other.

"But the net result is that we are imposing tyranny on each other, often in defiance of the *Constitution* and the guarantees in the *Bill of Rights*, and we create bureaucracies to manage and enforce our rules and these bureaucracies *benefit* from the existence of these new rules, these new laws. And, no matter how unconstitutional they may be, soon the bureaucrats themselves will fight to keep bad laws in place, even when you and I have seen the light and want those laws repealed."

"Have you got specific examples of this?" Dave asked.

"I gave you some: zoning laws, blue laws, speech laws, campaign finance laws, but the example you can learn the most from is the War on Drugs because, in the beginning, I don't think anyone foresaw where it would lead us.

"Drug laws started out as tax laws not long after the turn of the century. But we need to fast forward to 1934, when Prohibition was repealed, to see how they got worse. When Prohibition ended, there was the question of what the government was going to do with all the agents it had hired to run down the bootleggers, speakeasy

> ### Amendment IX
> The enumeration in the Constitution, of certain rights, shall not be construed to deny or disparage others retained by the people.

owners, and rumrunners. The obvious answer was to send them home. But FDR was too *kind hearted* to throw anyone out of work once they were living off the largess of the taxpayers, even though, in his election campaign, he had sworn he was going to cut the size of government. So he set this crew off to chase drug users.

"It was a practical decision. Prohibition had failed because it had been imposed on whites; whites wanted to drink so whites ended it. But whites didn't do drugs. Only blacks and Mexicans did. So Roosevelt turned the otherwise idle agents of the war on alcohol to pursuing drugs, and the rest was history."

"That sounds like blatant racism," Dave said.

"It was. Of course, no one foresaw the 1960s when white kids would start smoking pot, dropping acid, and snortin' coke the way their parents and grandparents had been swilling beer, wine, and bathtub gin. But suddenly, white America found itself throwing its own children and grandchildren in jails."

"You've said before that the drug laws are unconstitutional," Dave said.

"They are. The federal government has no authority to make such laws. The *9th* and *10th Amendments* to the *Constitution* make it pretty clear that we can do with our bodies as we wish. The *14th Amendment* says the states have got to leave us alone, too."

I grabbed a copy of the *World Almanac* from the bookshelf and turned to the *Constitution*. "What about the general welfare clause in the *Constitution*?" I asked.

"The general welfare clause is in the preamble to the *Constitution*. James Madison, the man most responsible for the *Constitution* and the author of the general

---

Amendment IV

The right of the people to be secure in their persons, houses, papers, and effects, against unreasonable searches and seizures, shall not be violated, and no Warrants shall issue, but upon probable cause, supported by Oath or affirmation, and particularly describing the place to be searched, and the persons or things to be seized.

welfare clause, said it is merely a statement of the intent of the *Constitution* and that the rules the government has to follow to carry out that intent, as well as prohibitions which apply to how the government is allowed to operate, are

> ## Amendment X
> The powers not delegated to the United States by the Constitution, nor prohibited by it to the States, are reserved to the States respectively, or to the people.

contained in the Articles and the Amendments. If the general welfare can be used to justify exceptions to the Articles and Amendments, and many Congressmen and their constituents believe it can be used to do exactly that, then it's the only thing that matters in the *Constitution*.

"Freedom of speech? Freedom of religion? Freedom to bear arms? Congress can then disregard them by invoking the general welfare clause. Want to be President for life? Invoke the general welfare clause and you never have to leave the White House."

"I see what you mean," Dave said.

"Why didn't they stop once white kids were being thrown in jail?" I asked.

"In a cruel twist of fate, by the 1960s the antidrug campaign had become a huge industry. There were people who benefitted from it despite the fact that it is illegal and was ruining millions of lives."

"Who benefits from it?" Dave asked.

"The livelihoods of police, bureaucrats, judges, lawyers, and many others depend on drugs being illegal and remaining illegal. And, like many other industries, the drug prohibition industry is a growth industry; it grows by making more and more laws which are increasingly pervasive and harsher and have less constitutional basis."

"Which laws?" Dave asked.

"Start with RICO, the *Racketeer Influenced and Corrupt Organizations Act*. When RICO was passed, it became *legal*, despite the *Fourth* and *Fifth Amendments* to the *Constitution*, for the police to deprive citizens of property without due process. They can do this simply on the suspicion alone that the property is linked to a crime. They don't have to have a warrant, they don't even have to prove their accusations. RICO is not only unconstitutional, it abrogates the body of common law and tradition our legal system rests on. The state no longer has to prove citizens are guilty of anything to seize their belongings; the citizens must prove they are innocent through an almost impossible and expensive process which includes posting bonds which, in theory, the government can also seize."

"But how does government benefit from these laws?" Dave asked.

"The value of many of the seized goods, including cars, homes, boats, guns, land, jewelry, and other hard goods, as well as cash, were supposed to be added to the budgets of various law enforcement agencies to help fight the War on Drugs. But politicians and other bureaucrats aren't stupid. Once they saw the vast amounts of extra money going into law enforcement, they weren't going to sit by without getting a slice of the pie. However, they couldn't just take it. They could, on the other hand, cut the budgets of law enforcement by the dollar amount of the goods seized."

"So police budgets didn't get bigger," Dave said, "the sources of their funding just got shifted."

"That's right," Mac said, "And what we have now are the police departments of America with an economic stake in keeping these unconstitutional laws on the books and enforcing them."

"Are they the only part of the government that benefits from the War on Drugs?" I asked.

"No. The same goes for prisons. If the War on Drugs were dropped and the P.O.W.s, the hostages taken in that war, were sent home, some three quarters of our prison population would disappear.

"You are aware that today the United States imprisons a greater percentage of its own citizens than any other country in the world, aren't you? So what would all the prison guards currently employed to do this do? Where would the wardens get their next jobs? What would happen to all those communities in the middle of nowhere whose main industry is the prison? As prisons closed, real estate would plummet in those communities and people would lose their life savings. Do you think someone with $100,000 into a house, in one of these backwater towns, wants the illegal War on Drugs stopped? Think about it.

"Then, how do you think lawyers would fare if drug laws went away? Have you ever stopped to think of how much of the legal system is employed prosecuting or defending people in drug cases? Even court appointed lawyers are on the payroll. How many lawyers would suddenly discover they can't afford to feed their kids if all the laws concerning drug and other victimless crimes disappeared?

"And the economics reaches even beyond them. It goes all the way to corporate America which manufactures drug detection chemicals and equipment, builds prisons, even makes uniforms. Many livelihoods depend on these laws, and the amount of money involved runs into the hundred of billions. It's more money than goes through any of the corporate giants in America today.

"People are going to prison, losing their property, having their lives destroyed, and sometimes they are dying because of these unconstitutional laws. And we all have blood on our hands."

He looked down at his feet, then up again at us. "Do you guys want to talk about baseball? Or girls?" he asked.

I laughed. Dave didn't. "I want to talk about this," Dave said.

Mac nodded and leaned forward. "Okay, but let me tell you something: The rights we bought with blood 200 years ago we now exchange for loaves of bread. As a friend of mine once said, 'the War on Drugs is nothing more than a Full Employment Act for lawyers, judges, policemen, prison systems, corporations, and their attendant bureaucracies,' and he's right."

"What about the people who give drugs to children?" I asked.

"Are you insinuating that children have become a rational basis for how we treat everyone else with our drug policies? Because we don't

> **Amendment V**
>
> No person shall be held to answer for a capital, or otherwise infamous crime, unless on a presentment or indictment of a Grand Jury, except in cases arising in the land or naval forces, or in the Militia, when in actual service in time of War or public danger; nor shall any person be subject for the same offence to be twice put in jeopardy of life or limb; nor shall be compelled in any criminal case to be a witness against himself, nor be deprived of life, liberty, or property, without due process of law; nor shall private property be taken for public use, without just compensation.

want our kids to have drugs, it's okay to jail every adult we catch lighting up a joint or snorting a line? If that's your intent, we don't want our kids to drink, so you shouldn't object if we use that logic to jail everyone who drinks a beer. And we certainly don't want our kids having underage sex, so your reasoning can become the foundation for throwing their parents in jail for the very act of procreation."

"Drugs are different from alcohol and sex," I said.

"Yes, they are, but the logic you're using can be applied to more than one case, and logic is independent of the subject content. This is something discovered at least as far back as the Greeks and it hasn't been in serious dispute among mathematicians or philosophers since."

Dave and I looked at each other.

"We're imposing this dictatorship on ourselves," Mac said. "And as we invest more power in the government, we not only get used to less freedom, but the government itself has more power to enhance and entrench itself. The result is that we have less control over it and it is less and less responsive to us."

"There must be a way we can change it," Dave said.

"We can change it. But to change it, we'd have to change ourselves, and I don't see that happening."

"But there's got to be a way," Dave persisted.

"I used to say we could change things at the polls, but I now realize we won't. Mostly because there just aren't enough of us who see what's happening to make a difference at the polls.

Jury nullification of bad laws

"But there's still one hope left. Historically, many bad laws have been countered in the courtrooms of America. It doesn't take a majority to counter bad laws there."

"Any specific examples?" Dave asked.

"Before the War Between the States, there was the *Fugitive Slave Act*, a federal law which ordered the return of runaway slaves to their *masters* in the slave states. However, the runaway slaves were entitled to trials and prosecutors soon discovered that, as the trials took place where the runaway slaves had fled—in the North—northern juries frequently ignored the law and voted their consciences allowing the slaves to remain free, despite federal law. It took only one person on a jury to hang the jury and block the return of a slave to his or her *owner*. This necessitated a retrial which slave owners didn't like. But more often whole juries refused to rule against the return of the slaves, making a retrial impossible and ensuring the slave could remain free. It soon became all but impossible to enforce the runaway slave laws, at least until the southern states had a federal law passed that prohibited jury trials in these cases.

"Another good example comes from our grandparents' time. Prohibition was repealed because again and again government prosecutors couldn't get convictions.

Amendment VI

In all criminal prosecutions, the accused shall enjoy the right to a speedy and public trial, by an impartial jury of the State and district wherein the crime shall have been committed, which district shall have been previously ascertained by law, and to be informed of the nature and cause of the accusation; to be confronted with the witnesses against him; to have compulsory process for obtaining witnesses in his favor, and to have the Assistance of Counsel for his defence.

Juries refused to convict bootleggers and speakeasy owners despite both the *18th Amendment*, which outlawed booze, and the *Volstead Act*, which put teeth into the Amendment. Both were the 'law of the land,' but they were laws that most of the American people knew were wrong. Individual jurors frequently hung juries and, in other cases, convinced fellow jurors to acquit the accused so there could be no retrial. Prosecutors finally stopped bringing the cases to trial and Congress and the States finally passed the *21st Amendment* which repealed the Prohibition laws."

"Why aren't we doing this in courtrooms today?" I asked.

Stacking juries

"One of the things the government did back in the 19th century to finally stop juries from nullifying the *Fugitive Slave Act* was to change the law so that runaway slaves could no longer have the benefit of jury trials. Today, our government has learned to get around jury nullification by barring anyone from juries who disagrees with the laws or who knows they're unconstitutional."

"Sounds like jury rigging," Dave said.

"It is."

"How does the government identify a potential juror who might nullify the law?" I asked.

"The government uses a process called *voir dire*. In French the term means 'to speak the truth.' They use it to interrogate jurors and get rid of anyone who disagrees with the law. There was a time when about all jurors were asked was their names and whether or not they could bring a fair verdict in a trial. Nowadays, *voir dire* is the tool the government uses to ensure that no one who would vote their consciences can be on a jury and that those who are left on the jury, though they may still disagree with the law, are compliant and will bring a verdict of guilt even when the law is outrageous or unconstitutional.

"Today it is often the only way the government can get convictions with bad laws. To those who think drugs should be outlawed, this practice may sound acceptable. But it's the equivalent of the government barring anyone who believes in the freedom of speech from a jury when it's trying to suppress speech or, if it wanted to suppress religion, barring anyone from juries who believe in the freedom of religion. And it's the same with drugs. Anyone who clearly sees this as a violation of our *9th Amendment* guarantees is thrown off the jury by a government employee, the judge. Only those who agree with the government when it commits illegal acts, or who will be compliant even when they know the law is wrong, are allowed to sit there. Does this sound like freedom to you?"

I said, "One of the times I was on jury duty the judge specifically mentioned jury nullification and announced to us that we weren't there to change the law. He said that's what we have the legislature for."

"Of course he did. By first tying the hands of defense attorneys—not letting them plead for jury nullification when the law is bad—then falsely informing jurors that they cannot cast their votes against bad laws in the jury room, government prosecutors roll up an impressive string of victories and make it appear as though they have the complicity of the citizenry when unconstitutionally destroying a defendant's life."

"What happens if the defense lawyer actually asks the jury to consider jury nullification?" Dave asked.

"He can be fined or jailed for contempt of court, he can be disbarred, or the judge can even declare a mistrial."

"Are many people likely to hang a jury or get the accused off in a drug case?" I asked.

"In public opinion polls, some 30 percent of people don't believe marijuana should be a crime. The state now goes out of its way to keep these 30 percent out of the jury box during drug trials. And as long as the citizens of this country are too dense to see this, the government will continue to stack the juries. And drug cases aren't the only cases they do this in; they do it in *all* of them.

> *The whole aim of practical politics is to keep the populace alarmed—and thus clamorous to be led to safety—by menacing it with an endless series of hobgoblins, all of them imaginary.*
>
> **H.L. Mencken**

"By the way, the government doesn't always have to stack juries to get convictions. There are many cases where you can be deprived of your property or be thrown in jail, but our government does not allow you a jury trial."

"Like when?" I asked.

"IRS courts do not allow a jury of your peers to try you, and many states and the federal government routinely deny defendants jury trials if the sentence that can be imposed is six months or less. They can do this even if there are multiple charges and the six month sentences are going to run consecutively. This way, our own government has found ways to put people away for years in clear violation of the *Fifth* and *Sixth Amendments* to the *Constitution*."

"You don't sound like you have much faith in the American court system," Dave said.

Mac leaned forward again. "If Christ had a jury trial in modern America, the judge would bar from the jury anyone who would vote his or her conscience, and he'd tell the remaining jurors they were not there to exercise their consciences, but only to determine the facts in the case. Under those circumstances, even Christians left on the jury would vote, albeit reluctantly, for crucifixion unless they're black."

Can blacks save freedom?

"What do you mean, 'unless they're black?'" Dave asked.

"White Americans are more apt to bring a conviction even if they disagree with the law or feel the law is unfair, unjust, or applied unfairly, than blacks are. Blacks often have first-hand experience, either personally or through family, friends, and acquaintances, with bad laws, unfair laws, and police lying—called *testilying* among the police. A black juror is also more likely than a white juror to defy the judge's instructions and acquit a defendant—even if the prosecutor proves his case—

when he disagrees with the law. Whites are more compliant when confronted by the law. It would be ironic if American freedoms were saved by blacks, the people whose families were so recently slaves, while white Americans continue to behave as sheep. The problem, of course, is that government's solution to this would be to choose jurors based on racial profiling, just as traffic stops and airport strip searches are based primarily on racial profiling.

"You make things sound like they're never going to change," Dave said.

"What about judges?" I asked. "Why don't they step in?"

"The judge can be your worst enemy in the courtroom. Judges routinely deny you the benefits and protections of the *Constitution*. For instance, if you're arrested on a firearms charge, say carrying a concealed weapon without the local jurisdiction's consent, you will not be allowed to use the *Constitution*, specifically the *2nd* and *14th Amendments*, as part of your defense. This is despite the fact that *Article VI* of the *Constitution* says, and the Supreme Court has already ruled, that the *Constitution* is the law of the land.

Article V

The Congress, whenever two thirds of both Houses shall deem it necessary, shall propose Amendments to this Constitution, or, on the Application of the Legislatures of two thirds of the several States, shall call a Convention for proposing Amendments, which, in either Case, shall be valid to all Intents and Purposes, as Part of this Constitution, when ratified by the Legislatures of three fourths of the several States, or by Conventions in three fourths thereof, as the one or the other Mode of Ratification may be proposed by the Congress; Provided that no Amendment which may be made prior to the Year One thousand eight hundred and eight shall in any Manner affect the first and fourth Clauses in the Ninth Section of the first Article; and that no State, without its Consent, shall be deprived of its equal Suffrage in the Senate.

"Judges often tell defendants they cannot refer to the *Constitution* as part of their defense and, if asked, they tell jurors they are not allowed to consider the *Constitution* in their deliberations. Of course he's full of it, but most people don't know this so jurors become willing accomplices with the state in violating the defendant's rights.

"Shouldn't the Supreme Court be deciding what our rights are in courtrooms?" Dave asked.

"I think the Supreme Court has done a lousy job of this, especially in recent years," Mac said. "More and more it surrenders our rights to government demands.

"The problem with allowing the Supreme Court to be the final arbiter and interpreter of the *Constitution* is that we now have a branch of the federal government deciding what the rights of the states and the citizens are. It was never the intent of the Founding Fathers to have any branch of the federal government, or any local government, decide what our rights are. And this is a power not mandated by the *Constitution*. Read it. Nowhere is it written that the Supreme Court can interpret our rights.

"It happens that in 1803, in the decision *Marbury vs. Madison*, the Court assumed the power to rule on the constitutionality of laws passed by the Congress, and I don't object to that. But we shouldn't depend on them to be the sole authority when it comes to our rights."

"Do you have a solution?" Dave asked. "Is there an alternative to letting the Supreme Court decide what our rights are?"

Article VI (clause 2)

This Constitution, and the Laws of the United States which shall be made in Pursuance thereof; and all Treaties made, or which shall be made, under the Authority of the United States, shall be the supreme Law of the Land; and the Judges in every State shall be bound thereby, any Thing in the Constitution or Laws of any State to the Contrary notwithstanding.

"Of course I do. I've always maintained that the *Constitution* and, at least, the first 10 Amendments were written so we could understand them. So if anyone should interpret our rights, it's we the people. The Supreme Court can still make rulings and pronouncements on the constitutionality of laws just as it does today and just as lower courts do during the appeals processes."

"You're saying we should allow defendants to argue the law of the land?" Dave asked.

"If they feel it's appropriate, and if they feel the local laws, or congressional laws, or bureaucratic edicts are are in violation of their rights, let them make their plea to a jury. Let them make their plea to the people. These are, after all, *our* rights," Mac said.

"You mean let individual juries decide the law of the land?" I asked. "I'd rather have the Supreme Court do it."

"No, let them decide the merits of each case. If the defendant and his attorney feel there's a constitutional reason why the defendant should be acquitted, let them argue it before a jury."

"Then why don't we do it?" I asked.

"Are you kidding? If the people started considering constitutional questions on a case by case basis, judges, prosecutors, bureaucrats, politicians, legislators, cops, and who knows who else, would tremble in their shoes.

"Unconstitutional laws would be unenforceable. Take the drug laws, for instance. Let's say someone is caught by the feds with marijuana. The defense attorney presents the *facts* to the jury. First he says, *Article I, Section 8* of the *Constitution* does not grant the federal government power to tell us what we can do with our own bodies. The *Ninth Amendment* to the *Bill of Rights* says we have certain unenumerated rights, and that medicating ourselves however we wish is among them. And *Amendment XIV* says that even the states cannot deprive us of our constitutional guarantees.

"Now, a good defense attorney is going to be more eloquent than that, but the fact is, quite a few juries are going to go into the deliberation room and wonder what right the government has here. They may not like drugs themselves. They may not even like the defendant or his attorney. But quite a few juries will see that the government is out of bounds and return 'not guilty' verdicts."

"What will this accomplish if it's only done one case at a time?" I asked.

"Prosecutors have a huge stake in winning their cases. They have limited budgets and their careers are measured by success. They will not bring cases to trial when they feel there's only a 50-50 chance of winning. They usually won't go to trial if they feel they only have a 90 percent chance of winning. They're looking for certainty. Granted, they'll take cases to trial they're sure they'll win and wind up losing them, but they wouldn't have taken it to trial if they'd known how bad their chances were from the outset."

"Then why don't we do it?" I asked.

"They don't want you to."

"Who's they?" I asked.

"Who do you think they are? Judges, prosecutors, legislators, bureaucrats, the FBI, the IRS...you name it. Quite frankly, they *like* the setup they have."

"What would be the net result if we, the people, insisted on it?" Dave asked.

"We'd have fewer crazy laws, law abiding citizens wouldn't fear their government or the bureaucrats, and we'd be freer. Freedom. It's all about freedom."

"Why isn't there a movement to do this?" I asked.

"Because, as I said, the American people don't want it. And, if a movement was afoot and caught the public imagination, the powers that be would marshall out their forces and predict doom, anarchy, and chaos. And we would succumb to it. And nothing would change."

"Worse yet," Dave said, "they'd expand the role of the juryless trials in our legal system."

Mac smiled. "You're becoming as cynical as I am," he said.

"Then there actually may be no hope," Dave said.

"That's how I feel."

"Aren't you afraid of stirring up some bureaucrat or some other powers and getting into trouble?" I asked.

"No," Mac replied.

"Why not?"

"Because no one is going to listen to me. You could publish stuff like this, but it would change nothing. That's how we're bringing a dictatorship on ourselves."

Dave looked up at the clock. "Well, let's see what you've given us so far: You've said we're losing our rights, we can't blame the people depriving us of our rights because we're doing it to ourselves, and we could change these things—some of them, anyway—but there aren't enough of us to do this at the polls, but we could do it in the courtrooms, but our government is already putting measures in place to prevent that. So, it's hopeless, and we have only ourselves to blame for it."

He stood up. "You guys want to head down to the local pancake emporium and talk about this over breakfast?"

"Sure," I said and stood up myself.

"You hungry, Mac?" I asked.

"Yeah," he said as he stood up and yawned.

As we walked out the door, Dave looked at his pad of paper. "Do you actually believe these new rights, these things you refer to as..." he looked back at the pad, "...legal rights are a step in the direction of a dictatorship?" he asked Mac.

"Sure. I'll explain it over breakfast."

And we went out the door. Δ

Part II

How the creation of new "legal" rights is destroying our real rights

We went down to one of the restaurants here in Gold Beach—Dave, Mac, and me. Dave, of course, is Dave Duffy, the publisher of *Backwoods Home Magazine* and Mac is O.E. MacDougal, our poker-playing friend from southern California.

That morning, when Dave and I arrived at the office, we found Mac sleeping on the floor. Mac said he'd arrived at about two in the morning and he had let himself in.

Somehow or other, while we were still at the office, we started talking about possible catastrophes for the "end of the world specials" ad that, until this issue, we ran on the inside back cover of the magazine, and when we asked Mac if he could suggest another scenario he mentioned what he saw as a half dozen signs that we may have an American dictatorship in our future. His reply came as a surprise to us and we asked him what he meant.

While we were still at the office he explained the first of those signs. He said it was the steady erosion of our basic rights—our natural rights, as he called them, and after listening to his explanation it is more appropriate to call them natural rights than constitutional rights.

When he had finished that explanation we left for breakfast and, now, seated at the restaurant, I was hoping he'd pick up the thread with the second sign of a possible dictatorship. But he and Dave started out discussing the merits of the different breakfasts on the menu—pancakes vs. omelettes and bacon vs. sausage. Then they talked about fishing here at the mouth of the Rogue River which lies at the north end of Gold Beach.

I listened patiently and thought they'd forgotten our morning conversation, but just about the time our breakfasts arrived Mac said, "You know, the second thing we have to worry about is how politicians, bureaucrats, and special interest groups have created the illusion that they can manufacture new rights—legal rights."

"What do you mean legal rights?" Dave asked.

"Well, on the one hand, we have our natural rights, many of which are listed in the *Bill of Rights*. But now we have these new legal rights which Congress creates at will."

"Rights are rights," I said. "What's wrong with having more rights whether Congress creates them or not?"

Mac took a bite out of one of his pancakes. "Do you know the difference between natural rights, which are our real rights, and legal rights?" he asked.

"We've talked about this before," Dave said.

"Yes, we have," Mac responded.

"Go over it again?" I asked.

Our real rights

"Let's first define natural rights. When this country was founded, the Founders believed we all share a certain number of rights. Individuals are presumed to have these rights and they exist apart from the state itself. This belief has become the foundation of our legal system.

"In virtually every other country, today and in the past, the assumption has been that the source of your rights is the government.

"But in this country, and only this country, our real rights exist apart from the country and from the government itself. It is for this reason, though most Americans don't seem to understand it, that when a

31

foreigner in this country is accused of committing a crime, and demands his rights—including due process—he's accorded the same rights as American citizens because our rights are presumed to be human rights and not reserved for Americans alone. The people who founded this country assumed them to have existed before the United States existed and that they will exist even if the United States ceases to exist tomorrow. In fact, they are assumed to exist everywhere, including in other countries. They exist in China where they are simply denied, they exist in every two-bit African or South American dictatorship, and they'll even exist if we ever go to another planet. It's a purely American belief, though unfortunately most Americans don't seem to be aware of it anymore."

"Okay," Dave said, "and these rights, the natural rights, are the ones listed in the *Bill of Rights*."

"That's right. But the ones listed there are not the only natural rights we have. Also included are the so-called unenumerated rights inferred in the *Ninth Amendment*. But, taken together, they are, as far we're concerned, the rights everyone is born with."

"But what's wrong with establishing more rights?" Dave asked. "It seems like the more the better."

"Yeah, the more the merrier," I added.

"What's wrong is that these new rights we've been creating since the 1960s have a cost associated with them," Mac replied.

"What do you mean, 'cost'?" Dave asked.

"All too often, when Congress, the President, or the courts propose a solution for some perceived problem, they create a new set of rights for some group, or even for some animal or object. And they pretend that these new rights supercede our natural rights. And, of course, as long as we're willing to go along with that idea, they do."

"Then you're saying," Dave began, "that when we create these new rights, we do so...," he hesitated, "...at the peril of our real rights?"

"Yes, that's exactly what I'm saying."

"Can you give me some examples of legal rights that conflict with our real rights?" Dave asked.

"Legal" rights

"What comes to mind immediately are the *Civil Rights Act of 1964*, the *National Environmental Policy Act*, and the *Americans with Disabilities Act*. There are others, but these three serve as good examples.

"Each of these acts is an attempt to impose government solutions to problems—both real problems and imagined problems—in American society. But right from the get-go, each is essentially a fascist solution."

"What do you mean they're fascist solutions?" I asked.

"Yeah, you've got to explain that one," Dave said.

"Fascism is an economic and social theory that property, though privately owned, is subject to government control."

"Are you saying we're fascists?" I asked.

"Capitalism asserts that property is privately owned and privately controlled; communism says property is commonly owned and government controlled.

"All three of the acts I mentioned, the *Civil Rights Act of 1964*, the *National Environmental Policy Act*, and the *Americans with Disabilities Act* make the assumption that, even though property remains privately owned, it is to be regulated by the state. That's what fascism is.

"Accordingly, each of these acts has generally been used to deny us our property rights, but lately they've also been used to deny us free speech and due process, and they've even been used to create criminal acts where there was virtually no criminal intent. They have also been used to create administrative crimes, which apply to land owners, small businesses, and corporations where the crime is often just filling out forms incorrectly or filing them late.

"Each of these, though legislated by the Congress and signed into law by Presidents, is in violation of *Article I, Section 8*; and of the *Fourth, Ninth*, and *Tenth Amendments*. But today, politicians, bureaucrats, and special interest groups feel that when they disagree with the *Constitution* they can safely reinterpret it or ignore it altogether. But the *Constitution* is the law of the land."

"So these things are all happening at the federal level," Dave said.

"No, even at the local level, new legal rights have been created by local governments which deprive you of your rights."

"Like what?" Dave asked.

"Rent controls which deny property owners the full value of private property, hiring practices which deny business owners the freedom to hire as they see fit, which is usually to hire the most qualified people, zoning laws which deny you the right to use your private property as you wish, laws that require businesses to provide access for the disabled, and many other things."

Civil Rights Act of 1964

"But the *Civil Rights Act* was needed to help blacks in the South," I said.

"And what did blacks get with these new legal rights? If you think about it, these new rights are rights granted by the state—specifically, Congress—and can be modified or withdrawn since that's the source of these rights. We've also discovered these don't belong to everyone. You have to belong to a specially favored group for them to apply to you. But the *Bill of Rights* belongs to everyone, even foreigners.

"But the worst is that now that our natural rights have become corrupted, the real rights blacks and other minorities got are the same corrupted rights we all now have. The *Civil Rights Act of 1964* actually brought them less than they were gaining on their own."

"But they needed a solution to the problem," I said.

"There was a solution."

"What?"

"The *Civil Rights Act of 1866*."

"What was that?" Dave asked.

THE CIVIL RIGHTS ACT OF 1866
Act of April 9, 1866

An Act to protect all Persons in the United States in their Civil Rights, and furnish the Means of their Vindication.

Be it enacted by the Senate and House of Representatives of the United States of America in Congress assembled, That all persons born in the United States and not subject to any foreign power, excluding Indians not taxed, are hereby declared to be citizens of the United States; and such citizens, of every race and color, without regard to any previous condition of slavery or involuntary servitude, except as a punishment for crime whereof the party shall have been duly convicted, shall have the same right, in every State and Territory in the United States, to make and enforce contracts, to sue, be parties, and give evidence, to inherit, purchase, lease, sell, hold, and convey real and personal property, and to full and equal benefit of all laws and proceedings for the security of person and property, as is enjoyed by white citizens, and shall be subject to like punishment, pains, and penalties, and to none other, any law, statute, ordinance, regulation, or custom, to the contrary notwithstanding.

"It was an attempt, after the Civil War, to ensure that blacks would not be denied protection by the *Constitution*. Unlike the *Civil Rights Act of 1964*, the *Civil Rights Act of 1866* was an effort to extend natural rights to everyone. It demanded the same rights be accorded to blacks that were accorded to whites. Unfortunately it was passed and immediately ignored by the states, the courts, the Congress, and each successive President.

"The *Civil Rights Act of 1964*, however, wasn't about civil rights or individuals. It attempted to create new rights by stepping on our real rights and it sought to do this by creating a more powerful, pervasive government. Had the federal government, particularly the Congress and the courts, been serious about the *rights* of blacks and not the *power* of government, they would have enforced the Act of 1866.

"But the Congress and then President Lyndon Johnson sniffed out a chance to follow in FDR's footsteps and enhance the power of the federal government."

"But didn't it result in more freedoms for blacks?" I asked.

"I don't think so. The *Civil Rights Act of 1866* didn't work because the American people didn't stand behind it. In the same way, the *Eighteenth Amendment* and the *Volstead Act*, which brought on Prohibition, didn't work because people really wanted to drink so they flouted the law. The War on Drugs isn't working for the same reason. And if the country wasn't ready to end segregation in the latter part of the 20th century, no number of laws could have brought it about. That includes the *Civil Rights Act of 1964*. On the other hand, when we are ready for something, or when the American people want something, no number of laws can stop it."

I know I looked perplexed.

"I'm saying," Mac continued, "segregation actually ended because blacks took a stand and enough whites took their side. It was that and nothing more. The end of segregation was already underway in 1964 when the *Civil Rights Act* of that year was passed, and to say it was the result of that Act is demeaning to those who actually brought it on."

"You're saying that the *Civil Rights Act of 1964* was the result of an upwell that was going to make a dent in segregation and not that the end of segregation came about as a result of that Act," Dave said.

"Yes. The color barrier broke in baseball in 1947, and the Birmingham bus boycott that swirled around Rosa Parks and Reverend Martin Luther King preceded the Act by nine years. There were thousands of instances of blacks and many whites ignoring the color barrier. Had blacks not taken a stand after World War II, and had not more and more whites given them support, the *Civil Rights Act of 1964* would have meant nothing. It wouldn't even have been considered in Congress.

"But the fact is, with or without the *Civil Rights Act*, segregation was going to end in this country just as it had been ending all over the world."

"Well," Dave said, "If things only happen when we're ready for them and not as a result of the laws Congress is passing, couldn't you say that there couldn't be a coming American dictatorship unless Americans are ready for one—ready to comply with one?"

Mac just nodded. and took a bite of a piece of sausage.

"Then that's exactly what you think. You think a dictatorship will happen because of what we're doing, don't you."

He nodded again. "We're putting everything in place for it because we no longer value freedom the way our forefathers did."

"Wait!" I said. "We still need the government to look out for minorities, the poor, the handicapped, and...and..." My arms swirled around as I tried to think of other groups I thought needed government protection. "They have rights," I said and ended my outburst.

Mac said, "The economist Walter Williams sums these rights up succinctly. He has said the so-called rights we have manufactured since the 1960s are not really rights, they are wishes. The right to health care, work, food, and the right of the handicapped to access, along with all of the other rights we have manufactured, are just wishes. Noble wishes, he asserts, and it would be nice if all these things just existed, free, as the right to speech, worship, and the right to keep and bear arms exist. But the right to free speech means just that, that each of us has the right to speak. But it doesn't mean someone else has to supply you with a microphone, megaphone, or even a soapbox to stand on. In the same way, the right to freedom of worship doesn't mean the state has to build you a church or subsidize your religious beliefs. And the right to bear arms doesn't mean the state has to buy you your rifle or a handgun.

"But those who advocate we all have a right to a job mean someone else has to supply you with an income. The right to health care means someone has to provide medical care if you can't afford it. The right to food means someone must provide you with food if you can't afford it, the right to housing..."

"These are the things that are welfare," Dave said.

"That's right. And, as Williams points out, it's not just welfare for the poor that's being forced on us. There's also corporate welfare in the form of subsidies, tariffs, and protections against competition.

"And the people who cry out for all of these things believe they are entitled to them, and Congressmen, to win your vote, comply and try to provide them. But not only do these new rights not appear in the *Bill of Rights*, it turns out they have to be provided by someone else, and the power to force one citizen to provide them for another, also does not appear in the *Constitution*."

"What about a black man's right to eat in a restaurant?" I asked.

"He doesn't have it," Mac said.

"That's a terrible thing to say," I said.

"Of course it's terrible," Mac replied. "And I wouldn't eat in a restaurant that discriminated against blacks. But by virtue of being black a man doesn't have rights to my property, my money, or my time anymore than by virtue of being white do I have any rights to a black man's property, his money, or his time."

"You're on thin ice here," I said. "You're advocating discrimination."

"No, I'm not. I'm saying anyone who wants to discriminate has the right to. But I'm not saying I condone it. However, we have a government that not only condones it, it encourages it."

"How can you say that?" I asked.

"What do you think Affirmative Action is? Despite its so-called intent to level the playing field by establishing de facto hiring quotas, it advocates what its detractors call 'reverse discrimination.'"

I shook my head. I simply didn't agree.

Dave took a drink of his coffee and leaned back in his chair. "So, it's a real right if it doesn't have to be provided by anyone," he said.

"Yes, none of your natural rights have to be supplied to you by anyone else with the exception of one, and that's the right to a trial before a jury of your peers."

Dave thought about that. Then he said, "And the right to a jury trial is there only because your fellow citizens owe you something before they're allowed to take away your freedom, your property, or your life."

"It's more than that. Our forefathers demanded that when the state claims it has a reason to deprive someone of their freedom, their property, or their life, we the citizens have the right to examine the case and determine whether or not it should be allowed."

"Why?" I asked.

"Because *we* may be next. Jury trials are one more attempt by the citizens to prevent government excesses. Or at least that's the way it's supposed to work. But nowadays, with asset forfeiture and bureaucratic edicts from the EPA, the IRS, OSHA, and other agencies, the right to due process has often been suspended or superceded."

We didn't say anything for a moment and the waitress came back and topped off our coffees.

"When a politician makes a promise to provide a new right, whether it's access for the handicapped, tenants' rights, animals' rights, or whatever, though he appears to be generous he isn't being generous at all. All he's done is thought of someone else who either has to supply that right or foot the bill, because he's certainly not going to supply it himself. And, the problem is, once he imposes that burden on someone else, he has in fact violated that person's real rights.

"And that's why you won't call them real rights," Dave said.

"Yes."

"But what about those less fortunate than ourselves?" I asked.

Mac took another bite of his pancakes while he considered my question. "Are you implying that if someone is unfortunate that I am obligated to assist that person?"

"Yes," I said.

Article I, Section 8

The Congress shall have Power To lay and collect Taxes, Duties, Imposts and Excises, to pay the Debts and provide for the common Defence and general Welfare of the United States; but all Duties, Imposts and Excises shall be uniform throughout the United States;

To borrow Money on the credit of the United States;

To regulate Commerce with foreign Nations, and among the several States, and with the Indian Tribes;

To establish an uniform Rule of Naturalization, and uniform Laws on the subject of Bankruptcies throughout the United States;

To coin Money, regulate the Value thereof, and of foreign Coin, and fix the Standard of Weights and Measures;

To provide for the Punishment of counterfeiting the Securities and current Coin of the United States;

To establish Post Offices and post Roads;

To promote the Progress of Science and useful Arts, by securing for limited Times to Authors and Inventors the exclusive Right to their respective Writings and Discoveries;

To constitute Tribunals inferior to the supreme Court;

To define and punish Piracies and Felonies committed on the high Seas, and Offences against the Law of Nations;

To declare War, grant Letters of Marque and Reprisal, and make Rules concerning Captures on Land and Water;

"And, if I refuse, I should be fined, have my property seized, go to jail, or be killed?"

"No."

"Then how are you going to make me supply those 'rights' to the less fortunate if I refuse to?"

No one said anything until I finally said, "There must be some kind of provision in the *Constitution* for taking care of the poor and the unfortunate."

To raise and support Armies, but no Appropriation of Money to that Use shall be for a longer Term than two Years;

To provide and maintain a Navy;

To make Rules for the Government and Regulation of the land and naval Forces;

To provide for calling forth the Militia to execute the Laws of the Union, suppress Insurrections and repel Invasions;

To provide for organizing, arming, and disciplining, the Militia, and for governing such Part of them as may be employed in the Service of the United States, reserving to the States respectively, the Appointment of the Officers, and the Authority of training the Militia according to the discipline prescribed by Congress;

To exercise exclusive Legislation in all Cases whatsoever, over such District (not exceeding ten Miles square) as may, by Cession of particular States, and the Acceptance of Congress, become the Seat of the Government of the United States, and to exercise like Authority over all Places purchased by the Consent of the Legislature of the State in which the Same shall be, for the Erection of Forts, Magazines, Arsenals, dock-Yards, and other needful Buildings;--And

To make all Laws which shall be necessary and proper for carrying into Execution the foregoing Powers, and all other Powers vested by this Constitution in the Government of the United States, or in any Department or Officer thereof.

"The Founding Fathers never made provisions for the federal government to have the power to trample our natural rights for the sake of what today's liberals call 'social justice.'"

"There should be," I said.

"But the fact is, they didn't, and trying to impose the responsibility for providing those rights is illegal under our *Constitution*."

"Why didn't they provide them?" Dave asked.

"There is no way to provide them without force and the people who founded this country didn't trust government. They didn't want to give it that much power. They believed that allowing the government these powers, for some imagined social good, was a mistake because once we grant it the power to suspend or negate our rights, the danger is that that power will never be relinquished and it will eventually be expanded."

Environmentalism

"You said the *National Environmental Policy Act* also violates our rights," I said.

"I'm not going to debate whether the environmentalists have a point with their fears of global warming except to say there is plenty of evidence that they're wrong and there are many scientists who disagree with them and their conclusions. And I'm not going to argue with their fears of loss of habitat except to say habitats are always changing and we have to decide what we want; in other words, there are trade-offs to be made.

"What I will say is that their approach to solving the problems, if there are problems, is political rather than scientific and it conflicts with both our rights and the limits placed on the federal government in the *Constitution*. People are losing their property, losing their access to their property, and losing the economic value of their property illegally."

"Well, let's suppose the environmentalists are right," I said. "Is there a solution that you would think is just?"

"The simplest solution to the problem would be that property owners be compensated for the loss of their property or for the loss in value when the government seizes it or limits its use."

"That could cost a fortune," I said.

"Of course it would. But today farmers suddenly find out they cannot plant crops because a bureaucrat has designated his property as protected wetland or the home of some protected vole. For the same reason developers are denied the right to build on their property.

"There's even the 'reasonable bird' rule, called the 'glancing goose' test by its detractors, that says that if a passing bird could look down and wanted to land on your parcel of land, then your right to what you can do with *your* land no longer belongs to you. It's not the bird's right either because, just as the bureaucrats can deny you any rights to your land, they can also grant waivers. So in a neat trick involving the hypothetical bird, the federal government has gained control of your property, clearly in violation of many sections of the *Constitution*.

"If we want to let the environmentalists have their way, it has to come at either a financial cost or the expense of our liberty, and we've chosen to sacrifice liberty. But who cares? No one, apparently."

"What could you possibly have to say about the *Americans with Disabilities Act*?" I asked and reflexively rolled my eyes.

Americans with Disabilities Act

"First of all, I'm not responsible for taking care of other people, disabilities or not. That may sound heartless, but it's true. And I may be willing to help people, and I actually would, but it's not right for the government to force me to. It's not right for someone to appropriate my money, my property, or my time to force me to.

The *Americans with Disabilities Act* isn't about the disabled; it's about bureaucracy. When it was proposed, Americans had visions of people in wheelchairs or with seeing eye dogs as the recipients. But the law was written so intentionally vague that the fat, the ugly, and the drug-addicted can call themselves 'disabled,' and so accommodations have to be made for them. And generally, this is not at the government's expense but at the expense of other individuals, namely the expense of businesses.

"Its intent seems to be to empower bureaucrats, win 'feel-good' votes for politicians, and enrich lawyers.

"But its biggest defect is that it is one of the most vaguely written laws ever passed, and vaguely written laws are dangerous."

"Why?" Dave asked.

"Because vaguely written laws are the tools of dictators. Even if they aren't originally intended to be so, they will eventually be used to expand governmental power at our expense. Any law not written in precise language will inevitably be used against the people. I don't care whether it's the anti-terrorist acts, *RICO* laws, or the *American with Disabilities Act*.

"I wonder why anyone in their right mind would opt to put a vaguely written law, which later can be used for abuse, on the books? It's the responsibility of the Congress, the President, and the courts to ensure that no laws are passed that can later be used this way. But, more so, it's *our* responsibility, we the people, to object to vaguely written laws. But we don't. We're too caught up in what's happening on the latest sitcom, the latest playoff games, and the latest celebrity gossip to look at what's happening to our freedoms. And we are now reaping what we have sown."

"Which sections of the *Constitution* are they violating with the *Americans with Disabilities Act?*" Dave asked with a smile.

"The same ones they always violate: *Article I, Section 8*, which lists the only powers the federal government is allowed, and *Fourth*, *Fifth*, *Ninth*, and *Tenth Amendments*...at least."

"You cite that *Article I, Section 8* a lot," Dave said.

"Read it. It clearly limits what powers the federal government has."

"I have," Dave said. "It's just that you never hear politicians or bureaucrats mention it."

Mac shrugged. "Today, our rights are second to the environment, to how the state perceives the welfare of children, to the beauty of our neighborhoods, to the preservation of historic places. But none of these things are mentioned in our *Constitution*. Our *Constitution* is made up of two things, restrictions on our government—including the rules by which it can conduct its business, and the assertion of the existence of our individual rights and the rights of the states. In practice, we expand the power of government and restrict individual rights and the rights of the states. It is for this reason that our government is overwhelmingly illegitimate and most politicians and bureaucrats could be found guilty of treason."

"What if the government has to do something for our own good but is prohibited by something in the *Constitution?*" I asked.

"That supposes two things. First it supposes that the wholesale ignoring of the *Constitution* by government agencies in both Washington, D.C., and at the state and local levels has been done for our good. Second it supposes that, if there are problems that require attention, that there aren't better, but constitutional, solutions."

"But wouldn't it be prudent to compromise some of these things in the public interest to solve some of our social problems?" I asked.

"I'm glad you said that because that leads directly to the second thing I wanted to bring up. Let's say we compromise property rights for the sake of the *Civil Rights Act of 1964*, for the *National Environmental Policy Act*, and for the *Americans with Disabilities Act.* We set limits on free speech so no one is offended, set limits on due process for the *RICO Act* and the War on Drugs, we set limits on the right to jury trials for the sake of government efficiency and to save tax dollars. We do all this and more in the name of *public interest.* If we're willing to do these things, then we'll compromise everything else in the *Bill of Rights* in the public interest."

"I think you're overreacting," I said.

"Hate crimes, politically correct speech, and campaign finance reform are all compromises on free speech, made in the public interest. The incident at Waco and many drug laws are compromises of freedom of religion made in the public interest. Twenty thousand gun laws in this country are all illegal but were passed as compromises to the *Second Amendment* in the public interest. How much freedom of the press do you think *Time Magazine* and the *New York Times* are willing to give up if the government says it's going to start censoring and managing the news in the public interest? How much censoring is *Backwoods Home Magazine* going to tolerate if your local bureaucrat, or the mayor, or the local cops, or if Congress, or the President himself, say it's in the public interest?"

I didn't answer.

"Which of our rights are negotiable in the public interest, and which are not?" he asked. "The concept behind all of these compromises is that we are freer collectively if we have *fewer* freedoms as individuals.

"Of course, the people who really benefit from the compromises are the people who derive power, often in the form of employment, from enforcing them. This includes politicians, bureaucrats, and special interests.

"But for the rest of us there's a downside and it's that we now have politicians and bureaucrats deciding what our rights are. And if you, as an individual or a business, violate one of their edicts because you thought you had a right to, you may find yourself being dragged into court. They use our money—your tax money—to try you and you also discover that it is usually cheaper to admit to a finding and pay a fine than to fight them because, even if you win, you spend more to defend yourself than it's worth.

"The result is that they win one victory after another and they are shaping our freedoms. That is, bureaucrats using the *National Environmental Policy Act*, the *Americans with Disabilities Act*, the *Civil Rights Act*, and a thousand other laws to determine which of your natural rights, or constitutional rights, you can exercise, and when you can exercise them."

"Why not challenge them during an election? Bring it to a vote?"

"If a politician challenges these acts, the bureaucrats and the special interest groups run to the press, which is usually young and liberal, and which comes out and defends the bureaucrats. If you point out that the *Civil Rights Act of 1964* violates our real rights, you're a racist. If you challenge edicts of the EPA, you're destroying the planet or you're a greedy capitalist pig. If you point out that the government *forcing* one person to accommodate another is a violation of that first person's rights, you're...what's the new term?...mean spirited. And that's all people hear. A politician taking a position against any of these feel-good laws will be abandoned by his fellow politicians in a vote on the subject, and he'll be abandoned by the voters at the polls who don't understand the harm these laws do. So, even if it were left to a vote, we lose."

Who's to blame?

"Do you care to do any finger pointing?" Dave asked.

"The Democrats are leading the way in passing laws that shred our natural rights, but the Republicans are finding they've got to join the parade if they're to survive at the polls."

"What do you mean?" Dave asked.

"The Democrats pass an unconstitutional law and the Republicans oppose it, but when the next election comes around the Republicans treat it as the status quo. So, once these laws are passed, there's no one in government with the courage to repeal them.

"Then there's the press. They don't blow the whistle on these laws because they are largely Democratic-sponsored bills and the media is largely, by its own admission, liberal."

Dave said, "So you're saying Congress is partly to blame, the bureaucrats are partly to blame, the courts are partly to blame..."

"And even your local zoning board is partly to blame," Mac said.

"Zoning boards?" I asked in surprise.

"Most zoning and planning boards work exactly the opposite of the *Constitution*, and they therefore operate illegally. They operate on the principle that anything not specifically allowed is prohibited. Zoning laws are blatant manifestations of fascism; property remains privately owned but subject to government control and direction."

"Man, you see demons everywhere, don't you," I asserted.

Mac just tossed his shoulder and ate more of his breakfast.

"When you say fascism, you're not talking Nazis," Dave said.

"No, mostly I'm talking economic theory," Mac replied.

Dave nodded while he thought about this and then we finished our breakfasts.

The waitress returned and topped our cups again and asked us if everything was okay. Mac nodded at her and smiled and she started collecting the dishes.

Dave looked at Mac and asked, "So, are we heading to hell in a handbasket? Are we up the creek without a paddle? Is there any way to save ourselves?"

The solution

"The problem could be solved if the people so willed it. The problem is that they won't. The American people don't know what their rights are. They imagine they have rights they don't and they'll even fight for them. But they won't do anything to protect their real rights."

"It's that mundane, that we're losing our rights because we won't protect them?" Dave asked.

Mac nodded.

"What about the theories that the New World Order or some other plot is the reason why we're losing our rights?" I asked.

Mac shrugged. "I've heard them, but they don't matter."

"What do you mean?" I asked.

"If Americans demand their rights, no amount of foreign conspiracy, no existence of an invisible government, no preponderance of multinational corporations can stop us. But if we *don't* demand our rights, neither laws, the *Constitution*, the *Bill of Rights* itself, nor the deaths on foreign battlefields of a half-million men we have now forgotten are going to save them for us."

"Can we talk more about this at the office?" Dave asked as he got up.

"Sure," Mac said and he fished around in his pockets as he stood up.

"Oh, no, I left my money in my car."

"I've got it," Dave said as he scooped up the bill.

And we left to return to the office. Δ

Part III

The role bureaucracy plays in the destruction of the Constitution and the erosion of our rights

The three of us left the restaurant that morning. There was Dave, Mac, and me. Dave, of course, is Dave Duffy, the guy who publishes this magazine, while Mac is O.E. MacDougal, our poker playing friend from southern California.

Earlier that morning, while we were still at the office, Mac had talked about the steady erosion of our rights. Then we went to breakfast and, as we sat in the restaurant eating our omelettes and pancakes, he talked about how Congress' invention of new legal rights were, in reality, destroying our real rights.

I was thinking about this after breakfast as we got in Mac's car and drove south, back into Gold Beach on Highway 101, heading toward the office.

But, just as we came into town, Dave said, "Take a right, here."

Mac took a right and we were going down into the harbor.

"Where are we going?" I asked.

"I want to check out the crabbing," Dave said.

"Crabbing?" Mac asked.

"Yeah," Dave replied.

Mac seemed suddenly more animated and, after he parked, he sprung from the car. Dave got out on his side and they walked toward one of the buildings.

I stayed in the back seat of the car and waited. I was still thinking about our conversation over breakfast. I started thinking that there must be an easy way to have our natural rights restored and these new "legal rights," which are dispensed by the government, relegated to wherever it is they belong.

Soon, I watched as they came back to the car and, as they got in, Mac was speaking excitedly about the prospect of crabbing. "I've got recipes that'll curl your toes," he said. "Crab bisque, crab cakes, crabmeat salad, a crab pie..."

"Didn't I see this scene played out between Forest and Bubba in the movie *Forest Gump*?" Dave asked. "But they did it with shrimp," he added.

Mac ignored him. "I don't know why I haven't thought about crabbing up here before this," Mac said.

"We can go tomorrow," Dave said.

"But your friend said we should go to Port Orford."

"Then to Port Orford we'll go," Dave said.

"Tomorrow morning," Mac said. "Let's do it."

"Mac," I interrupted, "I have just one question."

"Bureaucrats," he said.

"Huh?" I asked.

"You were going to ask me why we can't just assert our natural rights and who has an interest in keeping the legal rights in place."

I was a little disconcerted by this statement. "Says who?" I asked.

"You've been quiet," he said. "I just figured you were thinking about what we've been talking about this morning and that that was what you were going to ask."

I didn't say anything for a few seconds. Then I asked, "Well, okay. So, how are bureaucrats involved?"

Dave looked back at me in the backseat and laughed. "Is that really what you were going to ask him?" he asked me.

I didn't answer.

Dave looked at Mac.

"It was just a guess," Mac said. "These things look spectacular when I guess right and no one remembers them when I'm wrong."

"Well? What's the answer?" I asked.

"I'd say that bureaucracies are part of the problem in the erosion of our rights," he began. "They're funny things. They've been with us, one way or another, since the dawn of civilization. But when this country was founded there were none of the extensive and pervasive bureaucracies we have today. In fact, there couldn't have been."

"Why not?" I asked.

"Bureaucracies are nonproductive. They can't support themselves. They need taxes, tariffs, and licensing fees to survive. Their size is limited by the strength and wealth of the economic base around them. Back then, when the nation was largely agrarian, there wasn't enough wealth to support a large bureaucracy."

He still hadn't started the car and he stared out the window at the seagulls that were circling over the parking lot. Suddenly, he turned the ignition and the car started.

"You know," he said, "there are enough protections against the abuses of bureaucracy in the *Constitution*, but we don't apply them. I sometimes wonder, if the Founding Fathers had had firsthand experience with the abuses of giant bureaucracies, if they would have cited them specifically in the *Constitution*. Maybe they would have used words like, 'Neither Congress nor the damned bureaucracies they create are allowed to...blah, blah, blah.'"

"I think we've talked about bureaucracies before," Dave said.

"We have," Mac said. "John even wrote about it," he added as he pulled back onto the road and we continued on to the office. (See the article, "Why bureaucracy will likely destroy America," available in *A Backwoods Home Anthology, The Ninth Year*.)

"Why do we have them?" I asked. "Do they have any upside?"

"Sure they do. Historians believe that some of civilization's most fundamental and greatest inventions and discoveries came about as the result of bureaucracies."

"Like what?" Dave asked.

"Writing, math, geometry, and accounting among others. Bureaucracies had to have ways to keep records, record taxes, measure out land, and such. As conceived, bureaucracies were intended to make things run smoother. But, being made up of people, they have their problems, the biggest being that they look out for themselves, first. And, like any other human organization, they want to grow and acquire more power. They also seek to squash threats to themselves, and those threats are sometimes just people who want to limit their power."

"But who wanted bureaucracies in the first place? I asked.

"For those who rule—kings, emperors, presidents, or whoever—they serve a useful function. One of the things rulers throughout history always discovered or rediscovered is that establishing a bureaucracy will enhance their power over both the populace and their political enemies. But, as I said, the downside is that the first thing bureaucracies look out for is themselves. Even at the expense of the country's welfare. Even at the expense of the rulers."

The China example

We pulled up in front of the office and got out of Mac's car.

"Do you have any examples of bureaucracies that sacrificed the well-being of their country for themselves?" Dave asked as we walked into the office.

"Sure. Probably every bureaucracy has at some time or another. But the most famous is probably what happened in China in the 15th century.

"For centuries, China was the most powerful country on earth. They had the people, the intellectuals, the wealth, and most of all they had the merchant fleet and navy to have ruled the world. They also could have, and should have, been the traders to discover the sea routes around the world."

Dave sat down at his desk and I sat at mine. Mac sat in the stuffed chair near the filing cabinet. He looked as if he could fall asleep. He didn't say anything for a minute.

"Well, what about the Chinese?" Dave asked.

"Oh, yeah. Well, while the Renaissance was blossoming in Europe, and just before the Age of Discovery, which was a European phenomenon, China had the world's largest sailing ships and largest fleet. They traded with India and the Arabs and sailed as far west as the east coast of Africa. There's even evidence that some Chinese ships reached the New World before Columbus did. China was poised to literally overrun the planet, and Europe and its people would have remained residents of a backwater outcropping that sticks off the butt-end of the Asian continent."

"Just look at a map of the world some time. Europe isn't really a continent at all. It's just the rugged back door of Asia. The perception that Europe is a separate continent goes back to the ancient Greeks. It's the way they saw the world, and we've retained their convention.

"But, anyway, had it not been for its bureaucrats, China would have become the predominant world power in the 15th century and there's no reason to believe it wouldn't have continued to be so to this day."

"That would have changed history a little," Dave said and Mac laughed.

"So, what did the bureaucrats do?" I asked.

"As the Chinese navy was on the brink of overrunning the world, in Chinese cities a new wealthy class was arising. It was a class made up of merchants and traders that created wealth, great wealth, and they were already getting the ear of the emperor. But, within China was a powerful force jealous of these rising powers.

"This was the Chinese bureaucracy and they saw this new rising middle class as a threat to their power and influence. Their solution for dealing with these upstarts was to use the still considerable influence they held over the emperor. They got him to forbid further exploration, to decree limits on how far traders—in fact, any Chinese ships—were allowed to go and what ports they were allowed to visit. Overnight, China turned in on itself. The world's greatest seagoing fleet suddenly became a coastal fleet. They erased what seemed to be China's destiny.

"What the Chinese navy had accomplished was astounding. But the bureaucrats had almost all of the records of their feats of navigation and exploration destroyed so it would not happen again. They were bent on destroying any and all threats to their place in Chinese society.

"The result, as history shows, is that the Europeans—in particular, the Spanish, Portuguese, British, and Dutch—became the world's great explorers and traders and, when you consider how small their countries were and how remote their corner of the world was, it's incredible how their power and influence expanded far beyond what one would have thought possible.

"And China, on the other hand, never recovered from that setback.

Bureaucrats rule

"But it isn't only in China that bureaucracies have wielded incredible power. Throughout history, the big names in history have very rarely been the true rulers of any country. I don't care if we're talking about pharaohs, kings, presidents, emperors, or what. And it hasn't been 'the people' who rule, either. More often than not, it's been the bureaucrats.

"Long before Alexander the Great conquered so much of the so-called known world, the various civilizations were ruled by almost invisible elites that were the bureaucracies. It's been that way since the first cities arose. And great generals, like Alexander the Great, understood this. Wherever he went, whatever people he conquered, he realized that the way to consolidate his holdings was to dispose of the rulers—the kings, the princes, the tribal chiefs, or whatever—but to keep the bureaucrats in place. They'd run things as they always did. He could then go on to conquer the next city.

"Great conquerors have understood this throughout history. Those who didn't had the shortest-lived empires. Those who did left their mark.

"Eighteen hundred years after Alexander, the Florentine, Niccolò Machiavelli, created a place in history for himself by writing a short tract titled, *Il principi*, or what we in the English speaking world call *The Prince*. What he expounded upon in the book was how a ruler is to maintain power, and among other things he discusses the importance of bureaucracies. He recommends that conquering princes keep the old bureaucracies intact and not try to replace them with another. He understood that the bureaucrats already in place already knew how to keep the society functioning and that they would also give their allegiance to whomever took power, as long as that ruler both recognized and protected them because, as I said, historically, bureaucracies' first allegiance has been to themselves and they will give support to anyone who will keep them in their jobs.

"It sounds as if, no matter what their drawbacks, bureaucracies are important to a country's power," Dave said.

Mac thought a second. "They're incredibly important to the ruling elite. If a ruler wants to ensure he remains in power, the best way is to install a bureaucracy, if there isn't one there already. And if there is one, it's best for him to make friends with it.

"What kept the pharaohs in power for 3000 years was not the power of the pharaohs themselves, but the hold of the bureaucracy on the Egyptians.

"What lent stability to China was its bureaucracy. Dynasties came and dynasties went but the bureaucracy never faltered. Even after Ghengis Kahn conquered China, the bureaucracy stayed in its place. And when the Mongol hoards disappeared, the bureaucracy remained."

"So, are you saying we need bureaucracies?" Dave asked.

> *Government is not reason, it is not eloquence—it is force.*
> **George Washington (1732-1799)**

Mac thought about this. "They have their uses. They do get work done that we need to have done to function as a society. And they're probably inevitable. What we want to do is control them."

"Wait a minute," Dave said. "What do you mean they're inevitable."

Mac sort of smiled. "Bureaucracies are incredible," he said. "If you study them, you begin to realize they come into being naturally. I don't think the first bureaucracies were ever planned."

"What do you mean they happen naturally?" I asked.

Bureaucracy evolution

"Bureaucracies are evolution in action. Whether you believe in biological evolution or not, what the theory says is that if an empty niche exists, something will evolve to take advantage of it. In biology, plants evolved to take advantage of the energy in the sunlight that falls onto the earth. Herbivores evolved to take advantage of the energy now locked up in the plants. Carnivores evolved to take advantage of the energy now locked up in the herbivores, etc. The theory's not quite that straightforward and simple, but you get the drift."

"Okay," Dave said.

"So," Mac continued, "in an extremely simplified example, according to the evolutionists, say a dog comes into being. Once it does, parasites will evolve to feed on it. Worms will infest its guts; fleas, flies, and mosquitoes will evolve to suck its blood; leaches will attack it when it's in water. Almost never will these things contribute anything to the welfare of the dog. They'll just live off of it because it's there, because it's a source of energy—a source of sustenance.

"Hundreds of species and virtually thousands, if not millions and billions of organisms if we include bacteria and viruses, will live off of this one dog. There may be a microbe or two in the dog's gut that creates a vitamin the dog can't fashion for itself, but by and large none of these parasites will contribute anything to the dog's welfare. They exist only because the dog exists. As long as the dog doesn't die, more and more parasites will evolve to live off of it until all the niches that can exist, because the dog exists, are filled.

"Now, imagine society in place of the dog. In this case, we have a productive society. Government will evolve and bureaucracies will evolve. More and more bureaucracies will evolve to suck off its lifeblood, and as long as the society doesn't die, the bureaucracies will abound. Some will be useful, but most exist *just because society can support them*," he said with emphasis.

"So you're saying most bureaucracies exist because they can, not because they're needed."

"That's more or less it in a nutshell. There's a small core of bureaucracy that society really needs. The rest is just there because society can support it."

"What part of the bureaucracy is absolutely needed?" Dave asked.

"Read the *Constitution* as it was originally written, along with the *Bill of Rights* and you can figure out what bureaucracies the Founding Fathers thought were necessary, and I think they were right. We need a legal system, a governing body, a police force, a treasury system, a core of military personnel, and maybe a little more. But not much more. The rest is extraneous and is not there *for* us though we pay their salaries."

There was a long pause and Mac looked like he was sinking into the chair. His eyes were closing and I thought he was about to fall asleep.

"But the rest won't go away," Dave said.

Mac opened his eyes and threw his hands up. "That's the problem. And, as Alexander, Machiavelli, and numerous others have understood," he added, "if the society changes, the bureaucracy survives. The durability of a bureaucracy is truly astounding."

"You mean, they just stay in place," Dave said.

"That's right. For example, when communism and the old Soviet Union folded, you're not under the impression that the bureaucrats went home, are you? They showed up for work the next day and didn't even bother to change their name plates.

"They may have been communists and Soviets one day, and their politics may have changed and they may have been Russians the next day, but they were always bureaucrats. And whoever is in power still needs someone to collect taxes and enforce regulations. And the bureaucrats will do this for anyone because once they stop collecting taxes and spending money, they're out of work."

"What about us? How did we get these huge bureaucracies in this country?" Dave asked.

"This country started out with very little in the way of bureaucracy. In 1800, when the capital was moved from Philadelphia to Washington, D.C., all that had to be moved were 12 boxes of paperwork."

"And you're saying there wasn't much bureaucracy in 1800 because there wasn't enough wealth to support it," Dave said. "But as our economy grew richer, bureaucracies expanded."

"That's right."

"But, if they don't produce anything themselves, then all they can do is..."

"Regulate us," Mac said.

"Control us," Dave said.

"That's right," Mac responded.

"How can we change it?" I asked.

"We won't," he said.

"We won't?"

"No."

"Why not? Who wants them?" I asked.

"First, the bureaucrats want bureaucracies to go on. It's the way they make their livings. Second, the citizens want bureaucracies to go on even though they have a love-hate relationship with them because they've become dependent on them. And third, they are such a large part of our economy now that most people haven't got any idea how to get rid of them, or even just cut them back in size."

"Can you give us examples of each of these three cases?" Dave asked.

"In the first case, bureaucracies are run so they won't go out of business. In fact, the way some stay in business may be insidious. Consider the case of poverty in this country. I don't believe that any federal bureaucracy, from Department of Health and Welfare to the Department of Agriculture, really has an incentive to end poverty."

"Why do you say that?" I asked.

"Because too many bureaucrats now depend on the existence of a permanent underclass."

"What do you mean?" I asked.

"Most of the money spent on curing poverty is not spent on poverty itself, it's spent on the bureaucratic structure. In over 30 years, with over five trillion dollars spent on 'The War on Poverty,' the end to the problem of poverty is not in sight. I believe it's because nobody really wants it solved. If it were solved, all those bureaucrats would have to be laid off. They actually need the poor more than the poor need them."

"That's a pretty serious charge," Dave said.

"There's an antismoking ad in which supposed tobacco executives are talking about the number of people dying from tobacco related deaths," Mac said. "In the ad these executives talk about how they have to recruit more smokers from the ranks of the young to stay in business."

"I've seen the ad," Dave and I said almost simultaneously.

"With just minor changes," Mac said, "that ad could have been made about welfare. They need a steady stream of new welfare recipients to replace those who die or, worse yet, get jobs. I truly believe that the problem of poverty in this country cannot be solved as long as we have a huge bureaucracy that depends on the poor."

There was another long silence.

"But aren't there things we get from bureaucracies that we need," I said.

"I'm glad you said that," Mac said, "because that leads to the second reason we are becoming a bureaucratic state. Namely, we've become dependent on bureaucracies for things we should be providing for ourselves. Much of it are things we would spend our money on, anyway."

"Like what?" Dave asked.

"Retirement, for one. Health care is another. But let's consider retirement. The question is whether the best way to fund it is to run the money through bureaucrats, first. There is a question of choice and there's the question of whether it's cost effective."

"You're talking about Social Security," Dave said.

"Yes. But so many people are dependent on it today that no one dares touch it. Yet, Social Security is not only not an efficient way to provide for retirement, it is *grossly inefficient*. Not only do we only get about one eighth the return on the money withheld from us that we would get if the money were invested, but the money isn't even really ours."

"What do you mean it's not ours?" I asked.

"If you invest in a retirement plan and you die the day before you retire, your heirs get what you've invested along with interest it's accrued. But the money you've contributed all your life to your Social Security fund goes to the state the day you die. Your spouse may get some benefits from it while he or she is alive, but it's not something you can leave to your kids, your friends, or even your church. It's not yours."

"I see what you mean," I said.

"If we privatized it, the investment capital would enrich the economy and the largess from a life of working and saving would be passed on to our heirs. But the American people are so dependent on it, and so scared of change, that we are almost incapable of changing the system."

"So the whole Social Security system exists because *we* want it," Dave said. "In fact, because we feel dependent on it...even though there may be better alternatives."

"Yes. Social Security is actually a dismal failure. Countries like Chile and Great Britain, which have privatized their retirement programs, have not only seen booms in their economies once the money was invested instead of just being run through bureaucrats, but their retirement programs are on viable economic footings. You don't hear them talking about when their retirement programs go broke the way we talk about Social Security going broke."

I said, "Mac, you also said..." and I looked at a piece of paper I had made some notes on, "that some parts of the bureaucracy are 'such a large part of our economy now that most people haven't got any idea how to get rid of them or, or even just cut them back in size.'"

"Bureaucracies are a huge part of our economy. They not only spend tax money on themselves, but funnel a huge part of what they get through the private sector which supports them. Good examples are the defense contractors and the military. The military is essentially a bureaucracy, so the civil servants who support them, and the defense contractors who support the civil servants, as well as all of the builders of ships, planes, and bombs, are in favor of a huge military bureaucracy.

"When we talk about cutting that bureaucracy, i.e., defense, we're talking about a bureaucracy that reaches right into our own corporations and jobs."

"Can't we just cut taxes?" I asked. "That would cut their lifeblood."

"Presidents campaign on tax reform," Mac said. "They swear they'll cut taxes and make government smaller. But they can't. And the sad truth is, they know they can't."

"Why do you say that?" I asked.

"First, they can't cut taxes because so much of the money is now 'promised.' Americans have come to depend on big government, and when Americans say they want taxes cut, what they mean is they want *their own* taxes cut. But they still want government to cater to them. They just want someone else to pick up the tab."

"What part of the budget is promised?" I asked.

"The federal budget, right now, is about $1.8 trillion. Most of it is already spoken for. There are just seven items that make up about 75 percent of the federal budget, and it's the 75 percent that Americans feel can't be cut. Social Security is $403 billion, Medicare is $199 billion, Medicaid is $117 billion, military and civil service pensions together are $79 billion, defense is $294 billion, and interest on the National Debt is $220 billion. And with baby boomers heading for retirement and age related medical problems, some of these figures are going to explode. Throw in a few more of the so-called entitlement programs and less than one sixth of the federal budget is something that can be cut. This would be money for school loans, science (including the space program), and stuff like that. But, as I said, with Baby Boomers heading toward retirement, that 'promised' money is going to get bigger. More and more of the money going into the federal coffers will be obligated until one day there will be no money to cut.

"In all likelihood, taxes will be increased rather than cut."

"How much can we increase them?" Dave asked.

"I don't know," Mac replied. "Already, some 43% of your paycheck goes to government at the local, state, or federal level either directly or in indirect taxes you must pay on goods passed on to you by businesses in the form of increased prices. Worse yet, companies must pass on the cost of complying with government regulations, bringing to more than 50% the portion of the average person's income that disappears because of government.

"There are enormous amounts of money tied up in what constitutes 'government,' and it's run through or spent by bureaucrats. There is simply no way we are ever going to shrink bureaucracy in America. Americans will just be too afraid to.

"And, as their roles grow in our society and our economy, their powers will become greater. Government is now a growth industry."

"So, how does this lead to an erosion of our rights?" I asked.

The erosion of our rights

"Because our government spends prodigious amounts of money it has to raise prodigious amounts of money. It depends on the bureaucracies to raise this money. The bureaucracies not raising money also need to have something to do; otherwise they'd all be sent home. I'm talking about the *EPA*—that's the *Environmental Protection Agency*, the *ATF*—which is the *Bureau of Alcohol, Tobacco, and Firearms, HEW*—which is the *Department of Health, Education and Welfare*, and others. It is in this raising of revenue and needing to find ways to regulate us so they can justify their jobs that bureaucracies come into conflict with the *Constitution* and our rights.

"I suppose there was a time when you could have said the United States was the freest country in the world. But anyone who makes that claim now would have to explain why the world's freest country now allows government agencies—the bureaucracies—to seize your money, and often your house, vehicles, and property, without having to show any cause, without the intervention of a judge, and without a trial before a jury of your peers, simply because you are thought to be dealing in drugs, which, by the way, are a medical problem and should not be a legal issue.

"Or they get you for having too much cash at an airport. Or for depositing or withdrawing too much cash to or from your bank account. Or even for playing poker for real money.

"They can seize your property without accusing you of anything, without putting you on trial, and without waiting for a court order or a conviction. Even hearsay from witnesses who either want to negotiate a lower sentence because they've been accused of a crime, or who want to pick up a bounty, is enough for the United States government, any of the state police forces, or even the local town or county sheriff to seize any of your property or take any or all of your wealth.

"The *Bill of Rights* is supposed to protect us from this kind of abuse but many bureaucracies are trying to free themselves from the bonds that the *Constitution* of the United States is supposed to shackle them with. They seek exemptions from Congress and the courts, and they often get them. There is not a bureaucracy created or bureaucratic power granted that I can think of which, though at its inception was conceived of to solve a specific problem, hasn't been expanded far beyond its original scope so it is now trampling on some part of the *Constitution*.

"Come on, let's hear more examples," Dave said. He was clearly enjoying this.

"When investigated by the *IRS*, you are now treated as if you have no constitutional rights. They seize bank accounts without substantiating their claims and they act as if you have no right to a jury trial before your peers. This is all in violation of the *4th* and *5th Amendments* to the *Constitution*.

"And, speaking of that, though there are no exceptions in the *Constitution* to the *4th* and *5th Amendments*, in most states, if you go to a juvenile court, the following constitutional rights are prohibited: They are the right to remain silent, the right to confront witnesses, the right to a jury, the right to a public trial, and the right to be presumed innocent until proven guilty.

"There was a time in this country when the people understood that every power conceded to the government, no matter how narrow and special that power was supposed to be, would expand. Today, bureaucrats and politicians say they want something just for one reason and once granted that power, it quickly expands.

"Taxes were supposed to be applied to only the rich, now they are levied on everyone. The *Racketeer Influenced and Corrupt Organizations Act* or *RICO* was supposed to be applied to only drug kingpins, yet it is almost never applied there, but instead is directed against the general population. Drug laws started as just taxes to control a few 'problem drugs,' but today it has become a federal offense for you to have in your possession a drug without a prescription.

"We give bureaucracies what we think are limited powers, but Thomas Jefferson warned that one precedent in favor of power is stronger than 100 precedents against it. By this he meant that you can say no again and again and again to the spread of government power and it just holds its ground, it doesn't retreat. But say yes on just one thing, and it becomes a new foothold from which the government will never retreat."

"Which goes back to your comment that they start out, ostensibly with the intention of solving some specific problem but their powers mushroom way beyond their original scope," Dave said.

"Yes, and the power they acquire and exercise often isn't direct and, because of this, they seem to get around the *Bill of Rights* because they get someone else to do their dirty work for them."

"What do you mean?" Dave asked.

"One of the ways bureaucrats try to work around the *Constitution* is to force corporations to do it for them. They have banks inform on 'suspicious' transactions, they have airline employees report people with 'too much cash'—in fact, they offer bounties to airline and airport employees and then seize your money without regard to either the *4th or 5th Amendments* to the *Constitution*.

"You can't even buy a large amount of paper with cash without Secret Service agents showing up at your door."

"Why?" I asked.

"Because, when you do, you automatically become a counterfeiting suspect."

"You're kidding," I said.

"No, I'm not. Jean L'Heureux, the guy who works on the other side of that bookcase had it happen to him back in New Jersey."

I heard Jean laugh. "They were at my door all right."

"When did it become the obligation for private businesses to spy on us for bureaucrats?" Mac asked.

"You know," I said, "to get back to something you said earlier, they tell you right up front that if you want to be at the airport, you're subject to their searches."

"And that is supposed to suspend your rights?" he asked. "So, if they tell you you lose your rights on federally or state funded highways, or you have no freedom of speech in federal buildings, or you lose whatever rights they want to take away from you in so-called federal forests or state forests, you're okay with that."

"No," I said.

"What if the federal government wants to sponsor a religion at airports, or ban 'unfriendly' newspapers at airports. You'd be okay with that."

"No," I replied.

"Then how do your *4th and 5th Amendment* rights disappear at airports?"

I didn't answer.

"Look, what we have to do is bring bureaucracies under control. Every new law that threatens to fine, imprison, or seize property is a law that must be administered by a bureaucrat. It is conferring upon a bureaucrat the power to terrorize us and, let's face it, just as cops will get lousy reviews if they aren't turning in enough traffic tickets, bureaucrats get ahead by *doing* their job. They will exercise their power to get promotions.

"That's how air and water quality standards get tighter and tighter to the point where, today, they make no medical sense. That's how, under *RICO* laws, more and more property and cash must be seized. It's why zoning inspectors will not give an inch and they deprive you of what you thought were your property rights because, otherwise, *they wouldn't be doing their jobs.*

"Historic preservation boards must appropriate the property rights to more and more buildings including private homes, or they don't seem to be doing their jobs."

"It's usually Congress that passes the laws bureaucracies enforce," Dave said.

"But it is bureaucrats on zoning boards and at the *EPA* who violate your property rights, bureaucrats at the *FDA* who violate your right to do with your body whatever you wish, the bureaucrats from the *ATF* who violate your *2nd Amendment* rights, bureaucrats at the state *DMV* who restrict your right to travel, and bureaucrats at the *IRS* who violate your *4th* and *5th Amendment* rights. The list goes on and on.

"Some of the regulations for which you or a corporation can be fined, or which can land you in jail, or for which violating them will cause men with guns to appear at your house, are not even 'published.' That is, they appear nowhere in the Federal Register or in any other public document where it would be possible for you to look them up. They are nothing more than interoffice memos among the bureaucrats themselves, but they have determined that you are responsible for them even though it may be impossible for you to have been aware of them. The *EPA* is famous for this.

"Perhaps in some other country these agencies would be in compliance with the law. But in the United States of America, because they routinely trample our rights, almost all bureaucracies are in violation of the *Constitution*.

"But organizations like the *IRS* need to be run the way they are, or otherwise they'd never be able to do their job," I said.

"I'm not saying that that's untrue. What I'm saying is that to run efficiently, they and other bureaucracies must use police state tactics.

"There was a time when, if a choice had to be made between personal freedom and the efficiency of some bureaucracy, the individual could be counted on winning. But nowadays the smart money goes on the bureaucrat.

"We were once the freest country in the world, but we are fast becoming a Third World country with a first class economy.

"The *Constitution* is not there to place limits on us. It's there to

> *A government is like fire: a handy servant, but a dangerous master.*
> **George Washington (1732-1799)**

67

place limits on the government, but every compromise is toward more government power. It *never* goes the other way. And every new law that threatens to fine, imprison, or seize property is a law conferring power on some bureaucrat, somewhere."

"What's the solution?" Dave asked.

"First, let's state the problem," Mac said.

The solution

"If a business is run poorly, if it makes mistakes, if it treats its customer poorly or won't sell them what they want with the quality it expects, at a price that's reasonable, it fails—unless, of course, it is a protected business. If a bureaucracy, however, treats you poorly or won't sell you what you want with the quality you expect, at a price that's reasonable, they don't go out of business. In fact, they can make it illegal for anyone who does give you the options you want to operate, as the post office did, or they can make you pay for the service whether you want it or not, such as has been done with public schools, Social Security, etc."

"Why don't we just get rid of the bureaucracies?" I asked.

"We can't because we won't."

"What's that mean?"

"Consider this: One in every six workers in the United States today is either working in government or working in an industry that closely supports government.

"Tens of millions of this country's population collect something from the Social Security Administration and that number is going to get bigger.

"Anyone who thinks bureaucracy is going to go away is dreaming or mad."

"Then there's no solution," I said.

"Of course there's a solution. But first you have to identify the problem.

"The courts have taken the stand that they are not going to position themselves to do the jobs of the bureaucrats, that the bureaucrats should know their jobs best. But the courts are shirking their real duty, and that is to see whether or not the bureaucrats, in making their rules, regulations, and laws are treading on our rights.

"They have no problem interceding when it's school prayer, sexual harassment, affirmative actions, etc., but they turn a blind eye to the almost unimaginable costs and restrictions placed upon citizens and businesses by bureaucrats.

"The problem, of course, is that the courts are, in the end, just another arm of the state staffed by political appointees and, worse yet, elected officials who read the same polls the politicians do when taking a position on something. In fact, now that I think about it, elected judges *are* politicians.

"I've said before that there is no clear connection between the people, those who are governed, and the bureaucracies. It was the intent of our Founding Fathers that in this country the individual is supposed to reign supreme and the government is supposed to exist for his benefit. The American people seem to be unaware of that.

"But there are ways to control bureaucracies and make them less of a threat to our rights.

"**The first way is to stress accountability. Bureaucrats have to be in danger of losing their jobs—or even going to jail—if they violate our constitutional rights.** The same way you can sue a corporation for violating your rights, you should be able to sue individual bureaucrats or groups of bureaucrats.

"**Second, decrees and regulations emanating from bureaucracies should require legislative review before they can have the effect of law.** Let bureaucracies submit the rules,

> *Society in every state is a blessing, but Government, even in its best state, is but a necessary evil; in its worst state, an intolerable one.*
> **Thomas Paine (1737-1809)**
> *Common Sense* **1776**

laws, and regulations they want to foist on us to Congress before they can be enacted. Only about one percent of the bills proposed in Congress are enacted, yet about 99 percent of all regulations proposed by bureaucracies become the law of the land.

"There's definitely something wrong with that picture.

"Third, bureaucracies should not be able to exist in perpetuity. In fact, before a bureaucracy is created, it should have stated goals and, if those goals are met, it should disappear.

"In fact, it should also be possible to make a bureaucracy disappear by referendum so that bureaucracies are directly responsible to the public."

"Fourth, and perhaps the most important step we can take to controlling bureaucracies, would be to insist on jury trials by informed juries when people are indicted for violations against bureaucratic rulings."

"Isn't an informed juror a juror who realizes that when a citizen is on trial, the law is on trial, too?" I asked.

"Yes. Judges routinely tell jurors that they cannot judge the law, despite the fact that they are legally entitled to. No judge can order you to find a defendant guilty when you feel the law is wrong, even when you realize the defendant actually broke the law.

"Fifth, when a bureaucracy accuses you of violating the law, the burden should be on them to prove you are guilty. The burden should not be on you to prove you are innocent."

"All you're saying is: the solution to bureaucratic abuse is to enforce the *Constitution* and the *Bill of Rights*," Dave said.

Mac leaped out of his seat. "Hallelujah," he screamed and people from the other offices came running into the room to see what he was yelling about. Δ

70

Part IV

How the expanded use of Executive Orders has turned America into a dictatorship in limbo

D ave, Mac, and I got back from breakfast, and Mac now slept in the big stuffed chair we have near the office front door while Dave and I worked on the magazine.

Mac is O.E. MacDougal, our poker playing friend who lives in southern California, and Dave is the guy who publishes this magazine.

For a couple of hours we were fairly quiet while Mac slept. People coming in from the other parts of the magazine tiptoed about. We all wanted to let him sleep.

Because we had just gone through deadline for the previous issue the office was slow and quiet, anyway. Even the phones seemed to have gone into slumber mode.

I sat at my desk and read from the basket that contains the new submissions while Dave went over cost figures for the issue that had just gone to the printer. There was little in the way of conversation, except for an occasional comment from me about one of the submissions or something from Dave about some business matter.

Suddenly a voice said, "Another thing we have to worry about are *Executive Orders*."

I looked at Dave and he looked at me. Then I peered around my monitor to where the stuffed chair sits. It was Mac.

"Do you want to sleep some more?" I asked.

He glanced up at the clock on the wall, then back at me and shook his head as he yawned.

"What about *Executive Orders*?" Dave asked.

"I was just sitting here, trying to wake up, and thinking about all the stuff we were discussing this morning. And *Executive Orders* are another thing that, unless controlled, carry the potential for a dictatorship in this country."

"What are *Executive Orders*?" I asked.

Mac stretched as he yawned, then he looked at me. "At the federal level, they're *Orders* issued by the President and they have the force of law. At the state level, they're *Orders* issued by governors and have the same effect in whichever state he or she is governor. But it's at the federal level that they're a concern to us, as they're very often the way the President carries out the law."

"Clinton's issued quite a few *Executive Orders*," Dave said.

Mac nodded.

"How long have *Executive Orders* been around?" I asked.

"George Washington issued the first *Executive Orders*, though they were called *Executive Directives* and *Executive Proclamations* back then."

"What kind of *Orders* did he issue?" Dave asked.

"Well, he didn't issue many, but among them were declaring a Day of Thanksgiving not long after he took office. But it was just for that one year. The holiday we now observe as Thanksgiving didn't become an annual holiday until 1863 under Lincoln."

"Well, if *Executive Orders* can be a problem, who was the first President to abuse them?" Dave asked.

"Washington," Mac said.

"Washington, himself?" Dave asked in surprise.

"Yes. And he should have known better."

"What did he do?"

"One of his *Orders*, or *Executive Directives*, established a dangerous precedent and though there were those who denounced the Directive and how he had overstepped his bounds, I'm not sure anyone saw it as a dangerous precedent at that time."

"What was the *Directive* issued for?" Dave asked.

"There was a war going on in Europe..."

"There are always wars going on in Europe," Dave said.

"Yes. This particular one was between England, Prussia, Austria, and Sardinia—Sardinia was a monarchy at that time and not yet a part of the country we now know of as Italy. Anyway, Washington's *Directive* forbade Americans from consorting or trading with any of the combatants. He said that not only would the United States not offer protection to Americans who did, he also threatened to prosecute anyone who did.

"Now, I'm not going to comment on whether the intent of the *Directive* was good or not, because that's not the issue. What is, is that he issued an *Order* concerning the way American citizens were to conduct themselves."

"What's wrong with that?" I asked.

"He had no legal grounds either in the *Constitution* or in statute law passed by Congress."

I must have looked puzzled because then he said, "The President can't just make up laws whenever he pleases. Making laws is Congress's job. The President's job is to carry them out."

"The President can't make laws?" I asked.

"He's not supposed to. However, under our *Constitution* he may

> *"The accumulation of all powers, legislative, executive, and judiciary in the same hands, whether hereditary, self-appointed, or elective, may justly be pronounced the very definition of tyranny."*
> **James Madison**
> **Federalist Paper No. 46**

73

recommend legislation to the Congress. He can even veto legislation passed by Congress, though Congress still has the option to overrule him with a two-thirds vote. But he has no constitutional authority to create it.

"Because of this, at the time Washington issued that *Directive* it was recognized as a flagrant abuse of the executive authority."

"In effect, taking the law in his own hands," Dave said.

"That's exactly what he was doing. And that's the way many saw it."

"So how did Congress react?" I asked.

"They later enacted laws specifically to support this *Directive*."

"I'm confused," I said. "If they okayed it, what was wrong with him issuing it?"

"Congress was establishing yet another bad precedent by allowing the President to create law. I'm not sure if they should have issued a reprimand or what, but they should not have let this violation of the *Constitution* pass. This is important because, as I said, under our *Constitution* it is not the President's prerogative to create legislation. That belongs solely to Congress. This separation of powers was intentional. Letting Washington create the laws he is supposed to execute is tantamount to letting the police create the laws they're supposed to enforce."

"Not only that," Dave said, "but we don't want our laws made by just one man. That's akin to having a dictator."

"That's right," Mac said.

"So, what should they have done?" I asked.

"Like I say, I'm not sure. But they should have made it clear that laws do not originate with him. Creating laws is Congress's job."

"Then what should Washington have done to prevent trade with the combatants?" Dave asked.

"He should have approached Congress and recommended such legislation. It's his constitutional prerogative to do so. And he probably could have gotten it passed. But whether or not it was passed, by doing it the 'right' way Washington would have complied with the rules of how this country is supposed to be run and he would have been upholding his oath of office, to uphold the *Constitution*, an oath which is mandated by the *Constitution* itself.

"But in this case he didn't and both he and Congress created precedents that have rung down through the last two and a quarter centuries: that is, the President issuing *Orders* without legal basis for doing so, and Congress rubber stamping them.

"And though creating laws this way wasn't repeated too often in the early days of our country, Washington's precedent has become a problem today as Presidents have asserted themselves with ever increasing frequency and vigor. Because of this, *Executive Orders* have become a tool that could be used to create a dictatorship. And I'm not saying their existence will force a dictatorship, but not stemming their abusive use right from the beginning makes their use to create a dictatorship more likely.

"Keep in mind that freedom has been rare throughout history. It's very fragile and, even today, most of the world's dictatorships are, on their surfaces, democracies."

"Well, the country was new back then," I said. "Perhaps Washington wasn't clear on the concept of how to use those *Directives*."

"No, he knew what part the President plays in our system of government. The rules are right there in the *Constitution*, the very document he helped draw up during the Constitutional Convention just two years before he took office as President. It was drawn up with a clear division of powers to prevent tyranny, and Washington knew that, too. And he wasn't just a delegate to that convention; he was its president. He knew what was going on.

"The only thing I can say in his defense is that he may have been shortsighted and perhaps he didn't realize his actions were creating an unhealthy precedent."

"So, what's the purpose of *Executive Orders* or *Executive Directives*?" I asked. "They must have legal uses, too."

"They do. They're lawful when they're issued in a lawful manner."

"Like what?" Dave asked.

"They're lawful when they deal exclusively with the Executive Branch of the government. And that makes sense because the head of the Executive Branch should have the latitude in how he manages his department. That first Thanksgiving Proclamation was really issued just to those in the Executive Branch of our government, though Washington realized his lead would be followed by many others throughout the country.

"They're also legal when they're faithful to the *Constitution*."

"Can you give us an example of an *Executive Order* allowed by the *Constitution*?" Dave asked.

"Sure. Issuing pardons. The *Constitution* provides the President with the power to grant pardons under quite a few circumstances and they are often issued as *Executive Orders*. For example, in 1868, just before he left office, President Andrew Johnson, the man who became President after Lincoln was assassinated, pardoned all of those who participated in the Civil War, in any way, on the side of the South. This included people like Jefferson Davis, the President of the Confederate States of America, and Southern military leaders like Robert E. Lee. Johnson's pardons angered a lot of people in the North, but they were issued in accordance with the powers granted to the President by the *Constitution*. And such *Orders*, though we may not agree with them, follow the letter of the *Constitution*. They're lawful.

"A third circumstance that makes *Executive Orders* legitimate is when they are issued to carry out statute law as passed by Congress itself. It is the President, as head of the Executive Branch, who is responsible with carrying out the federal laws passed by Congress."

"Because that's the President's main job—executing the law of the land," Dave said.

"That's right," Mac said.

"Did Washington issue a lot of other *Directives*?" I asked.

"No, he didn't. And neither did the next 14 Presidents. From John Adams to James Buchanan, very few *Directives* or *Orders* were issued. In fact, most of the Presidents in the 19th century were really just the chief clerks of the United States. They were there to do exactly what the *Constitution* charged them with doing—executing the law of the land. The people charged with creating the laws were those in Congress, and they were supposed to reflect the will of the people."

Lincoln's "dictatorship"

"Who's the President following Buchanan?" Dave asked. "You make it sound as if he's the one who changed things."

"Everything changes with Abraham Lincoln. When he became President the southern states, as they had threatened to do if he was elected, began seceding, starting with South Carolina.

"You can make arguments as to whether or not the southern states could legitimately secede. On the one hand, you could say that if the states voluntarily joined the Union, that when they voluntarily chose to leave they should have been allowed to do so. On the other hand, you can make the argument that once a state joins the Union, and accedes to the *Constitution* being the law of the land, it cannot leave without the consent of Congress. And there are probably dozens of other arguments that support either side of the argument. But that's not the issue here.

"What is at issue is that, when the South seceded, Lincoln chose, for the next two and a half months, to run the country through *Executive Directives*.

"And the problem is not whether we should have fought to preserve the Union. The problem was the manner in which Lincoln proceeded to conduct himself. He grabbed power, acted illegally, violated the *Constitution*, and essentially ran the country as a dictator without consulting the Congress or the people. And, because Congress, when they finally did convene, all too willingly acquiesced, after the fact, to

> *"He shall from time to time give to the Congress Information of the State of the Union, and recommend to their Consideration such Measures as he shall judge necessary and expedient; he may, on extraordinary Occasions, convene both Houses, or either of them, and in Case of Disagreement between them, with Respect to the Time of Adjournment, he may adjourn them to such Time as he shall think proper; he shall receive Ambassadors and other public Ministers; he shall take Care that the Laws be faithfully executed, and shall Commission all the Officers of the United States."*
>
> Powers granted to the President
> in Article II, Section 3
> Constitution of the United States

everything he had done, it became the model for future Presidents who justified autocratic rule by claiming 'war powers,' even when no declared war existed. He ran the country as more or less a dictator."

"In other words, if the South had to adhere to the *Constitution*, so did Lincoln," Dave said.

"That's right," Mac replied.

"But there *was* a war," I said.

"There is no war unless Congress declares war," Mac said. "That's also in the *Constitution*. And Lincoln hadn't convened Congress to do even that. In the two and a half months following secession there was certainly time to call Congress to convene, but he never did it, nor had he intended to."

"What did people at the time say?" Dave asked.

"He closed northern newspapers that criticized his actions. He even had editors arrested. And when the Chief Justice of the Supreme Court, Roger Taney, stated that much of what Lincoln was doing was both illegal and unconstitutional, Lincoln's response was to have a warrant for Taney's arrest drawn. And though it was never served, it set the tone for Lincoln's presidency: Those who pointed out the illegality of his actions became his enemies.

"Lincoln, the Great Emancipator, conducted his presidency like a dictator.

"The good news was that, after Lincoln was shot, on April 14, 1865, four years to the day after the South had fired on Fort Sumter—and he died the next day—Congress quickly moved to reduce the executive powers of the President. This was done, in part, as a response to the presidency of Andrew Johnson who opposed Congress's moves to punish the South for the war. And, like I said, Johnson issued an *Executive Order*, well within the scope of his constitutional powers, when he signed a blanket pardon of those who had instigated or participated in the war on the side of the Confederacy. It angered a lot of northerners, but it was a smart move that allowed the country to put the war behind it.

"As it was, wounds from the war lasted for generations. But had spiteful northerners had their way, and attempted to punish the South, we may have wound up with a guerrilla war that lasted generations."

"Would Lincoln have issued the same kind of pardon Johnson had, and pardoned everyone who fought on the side of the South?" Dave asked.

"It's difficult to imagine what direction the country would have pursued had Lincoln lived. One could make the case that he would have done the same things Johnson had done and tried to ensure the national healing. On the other hand, you could make the argument that he would not soon have relinquished the near-dictatorial powers he had assumed within weeks of his first term. It's just one of those things we'll never know."

"Did Presidents after Lincoln abuse *Executive Orders*?" Dave asked.

"Lincoln's presidency was the high point of power in the presidency for the entire 19th century. For the next 35 years Presidents more or less stayed within the limits of their offices as dictated by the Founding Fathers, though it's not clear if it was because the men we had serve in the White House were different from those who serve today or if it was because Americans were different back then and wouldn't have tolerated it. It's probably a combination of both.

Teddy Roosevelt

"But with the dawn of the 20th century, that all changed.

"Theodore Roosevelt took the view of an activist President and he exercised more power than any President before him, other than Lincoln. He issued more *Executive Orders* than all 25 Presidents who preceded him, combined. In his own words he called the White House a 'bully pulpit,' and he was intent on using it as such to force through his programs.

"His view was that instead of looking into the *Constitution* and the laws passed by Congress to see what he was allowed to do as the Chief Executive of the United States, he was allowed to do anything unless it was specifically denied to him. This was a whole new twist on the *Constitution*. It ignored the words of the 10th Amendment, which says, 'The powers not delegated to the United States by the *Constitution*, nor prohibited by it to the States, are reserved to the States respectively, or to the people.'

"One of the things he did that had never been done before was to create a national police force, the FBI, by *Executive Order*. It's something the Founding Fathers never wanted and Congress had always rejected the concept."

"Why?" I asked.

"They were afraid of a strong central government, and a national police force in the hands of the President was absolutely not something they wanted."

"Why did they let him create one then?"

"Though he had political enemies, Congress rarely tried to hold him to the description of his job but instead gave him a free rein in almost all of his actions."

"Aside from how they might have felt about a national police force, were the other *Orders* he signed for good things?" I asked.

"Does it matter? Good, bad, indifferent. Let me ask you: Should we excuse the police for warrantless searches whenever they turn out to get a guilty verdict? How about torturing confessions out of people as long as you catch a guilty person now and then?"

"So, you're saying...?"

"I'm saying it doesn't matter whether the cause is good, bad, or indifferent. There are constitutional procedures that are supposed to be followed, and making exceptions because you believe your current cause is 'right' is setting a dangerous precedent. Letting a President abuse his powers because you feel he'll be a benevolent dictator is somewhat less than prudent."

I didn't have a response for this.

"Was the way he conducted himself as President taken as precedent?" Dave asked.

"The two Presidents to follow him, Taft and Wilson, both issued numerous *Executive Orders*. And like Roosevelt they both issued more than all of the other Presidents of the 19th century, excluding Lincoln. But it was Wilson who used them more indiscriminately.

Wilson's "emergencies"

"In 1916, while running for a second term, he campaigned on a platform to keep the United States out of the war that was going on in Europe, though historians now know that all along he was making plans to get us involved.

"Then, just three months after his election, he began creating federal agencies. And I believe, other than Roosevelt's creation of the FBI, he was the first President to bypass Congress and create federal agencies by using *Executive Orders*."

"What agencies?" Dave asked.

"Among them were the Grain Administration, the Food Administration, the War Trade Board (though we weren't in the war, yet), and the Committee on Public Information. And, not long after we entered the war, he had rounded up those who spoke out against the war until some 5,000 people were put behind bars."

"People were imprisoned for speaking out against the war?" I asked.

"Oh, yeah. You didn't monkey around with the guy who had once been a college professor at Princeton.

"He was also the first President to declare a 'national emergency,' because of the war in Europe, then use the emergency to assume powers not granted by either the *Constitution* or Congress."

"But we were at war—World War I," I said.

"No. He declared the emergency two months before Congress declared war.

"But, as happened after the death of Lincoln, when Wilson was leaving office—in fact, it was the day before Warren Harding took the oath of office—Congress repealed most of the *Orders* by which Wilson had granted himself power.

"The next two Presidents, Harding and Coolidge, did their thing with *Executive Orders* without doing too much damage. Then there was Hoover. He gets knocked for doing nothing when the Depression started. It's a bad rap because, the fact is, one of the reasons the Depression got so bad was because he monkeyed with the economy more than he should have.

"He issued numerous *Executive Orders*, many dealing with the Depression, and many economists now say that it was because he would not let the economy straighten itself out, as it had after every other depression, that the Depression deepened and, of course, Hoover got booted out of office.

The endless Depression

"FDR, who defeated him in the 1932 election, ran on a platform of fiscal responsibility and restraint. But, in his inaugural address, he gave a hint of what he was about to do.

"In that address, after first extolling the virtues of the legislative-executive balance our government depends on to keep us free, he threatened to exercise his 'broad executive power' if Congress didn't comply with his program.

"He didn't bother citing the source of these 'broad executive powers.' He just assumed, like his distant cousin, Theodore, that he was allowed to do anything not specifically denied to him by the *Constitution* or statute law. Though even statute law would become suspect when, during World War II he threatened Congress that, unless they repealed certain legislation he felt stood in his way, he would assume dictatorial powers."

Dave looked real surprised.

"But that came later. However, in those first days of his first term, he was also the first President to use the word 'war' in referring to a domestic program. He said he was going 'to wage a war against the emergency,' meaning, of course, the Depression."

"Succeeding Presidents would, of course, wage 'wars' against poverty, and drugs, and almost everything else. But it isn't an accident that the term war is used, because it is by citing war powers acts that Presidents grant themselves these authorities.

"But, as I said, the broad executive powers he was alluding to don't exist in the *Constitution*. You can look. You won't find them there. And he didn't bother to consult with Congress. Two days after his inaugural speech he closed the banks.

"But Roosevelt had to force the issue so he could end the Depression," I said. "He saved capitalism."

"What are you talking about?" Mac asked.

> *Before he enter on the Execution of his Office, he shall take the following Oath or Affirmation:—"I do solemnly swear (or affirm) that I will faithfully execute the Office of President of the United States, and will to the best of my Ability, preserve, protect and defend the Constitution of the United States."*
>
> Presidential oath
> Article II, Section 1
> Constitution of the United States

"Well, we were in the throes of the worst Depression in our history, and Roosevelt had to do something to save us."

Mac smiled a little for a moment, then he stopped. "Franklin Roosevelt has several distinctions. Among them is that he served as President longer than any other man to serve in that office. Even more remarkable is that he never served even one day in office over a stable economy. He oversaw either a depression economy or a wartime economy for over 12 years. Imagine if Clinton's entire eight years in office were during a depression. Would you be saying that he saved us? Well, FDR served eight years, proposing one program after another and even threatening to stack the Supreme Court when they stood in his way..."

"Shades of Lincoln when he threatened to arrest Taney," Dave said.

"Yes. But not only did he never see a good economy during his presidency, many economists blame him for the Depression lasting so long."

"Why?" Dave asked.

"Consider this: if any of his programs were working, not only can you not explain why the Depression dragged on year after year, but you can't explain why it deepened in 1938, five years into his programs.

"He initiated scores of work programs and economic 'solutions' along with a couple of thousand *Executive Orders*, yet the Depression continued without the economy getting any better.

"At the same time, on the other side of the world, similar programs were being forced on the Soviet Union's population, and they were resulting in mass starvation. Of course, no one bothered to point this out.

"No, Roosevelt didn't end the Depression. Not only did he not end it, his meddlesome policies were dragging the United States toward the kind of economies we saw in Eastern Europe following World War II.

"What was he supposed to do, nothing like Herbert Hoover did and watch the country plunge deeper?" I asked.

"I told you, the idea that Hoover did nothing is a myth. He tinkered with the economy endlessly and had no more success than FDR would have later.

"And as I said, we would have been better off if both of them had done nothing."

"I can't believe that," I said. "A lot of economists have said what he did was necessary."

"But none of those economists explain why what he did didn't end the Depression."

"This isn't about the Depression," Dave said. "It's about *Executive Orders*. Can we stay on subject?"

Mac laughed. "Sure."

"So FDR started issuing *Orders* right away?" Dave asked.

"Yes, and he used as his authority the *Trading with the Enemy Act* of World War I. This despite the fact that that the *Trading with the Enemy Act* in no way empowered the President to govern transactions between American citizens within the confines of the United States, and that act was only enforceable during a declared war. In 1933 the United States was not at war with anyone.

"But three days later, Congress passed legislation amending the *Trading with the Enemy Act* and thereby not only authorized Roosevelt's actions but made all 'emergency actions' taken in the future, by either the President or the Secretary of the Treasury, legal and binding as long as they were made pursuant to the amended *Trading with the Enemy Act*."

"In other words, they took themselves out of the loop," Dave said. "There wasn't going to be any more legislative process when it came to the Depression."

"That's right. Rather than assuming their responsibilities, as spelled out in the *Constitution*, they gave FDR *carte blanche* powers not included in the *Constitution*. And those powers are on the books to this day.

"Roosevelt then went on an *Executive Order* bender and became the model for all recent Presidents who wish to trample on constitutional limits imposed on the President. In fact, most people seem to be blithely unaware that many of the *Executive Orders* passed today start out with the declaration of a 'state of emergency.' Go out on the Net and read some of the recent ones. Their sole basis for legitimacy is that the President has declared an emergency, whether anyone else sees it that way or not."

"And just as Theodore Roosevelt had issued more *Executive Orders* than all of the Presidents before him combined, FDR issued more *Executive Orders* than all of the Presidents who have succeeded him, combined, so far."

"All the Presidents from Truman to Clinton?" Dave asked.

Mac nodded.

"Did he ever trample on the *Bill of Rights* with *Executive Orders?*" Dave asked.

"Of course he did. He seized businesses before this country entered World War II to settle labor disputes. Supposedly, this was done to help battle the Depression and to prepare for World War II. Meanwhile, the Depression dragged on. And nowhere in the *Constitution* is there a phrase allowing the President to seize private property."

"But what about private rights? Did he issue any *Orders* that took away personal rights?" I asked.

"Businesses are private property. Seizing them was an infringement on our rights. But his most infamous *Order*, and the most infamous *Executive Order* until John Kennedy took office, was E.O. 9066. It authorized the United States government to round up American citizens of Japanese descent, in a direct violation of their constitutional rights, and throw them into the most recent version of American concentration camps."

"What do you mean 'most recent version of concentration camp?'" I asked.

"Well, since we first started forcibly moving Indians onto reservation."

"You're calling Indian reservations concentration camps?" I asked.

Mac didn't say anything for a moment. He stifled another yawn. Then he said, "*The Northwest Ordinance of 1787* promised that the Indians would live undisturbed on lands west of the Appalachians. The Ordinance became embodied in one of the first acts of Congress under the new *Constitution*, in 1789. Of course, both the Ordinance and the declaration of Congress contained loopholes for us to unilaterally change things and, with the *Indian Removal Act of 1830*, we acted on these loopholes and systematically began pushing the Indians onto reservations to which they were to be confined. This country is now dotted with them."

"I still wouldn't call them concentration camps," I said. "We usually think of concentration camps in reference to the Nazis in Germany during World War II."

Dave had grabbed the dictionary and was looking through it. Suddenly he said, "Well, according to the *Merriam-Webster Dictionary*, the term 'concentration camp' entered our language long before World War II. It says 1901. So the Nazis didn't invent them." Then he slammed the book shut and put it down. "But this isn't about Indians, either," he said. "It's about *Executive Orders*. I want to hear more about them.

FDR attacks the Court

Mac yawned again. But this time he had trouble stifling it.

"Did anyone do anything to stop FDR?" Dave asked.

"The Supreme Court tried to when they ruled several pieces of New Deal legislation unconstitutional, and that's when Roosevelt threatened to stack the Court."

"What do you mean by stack it?" I asked.

"He was annoyed that the Court was overruling his Acts and he proposed to Congress that they pass a bill that would let him appoint extra judges. He wanted just enough to offset the judges that opposed his programs."

"Can Congress change the number of judges that sit on the Court?" I asked in a surprised voice.

"There is nothing in the *Constitution* fixing the number of judges on the Court. That number is determined by Congress. It had varied between six and ten until the current number of nine was set in 1869, and it hasn't been changed since."

"So, what happened?"

"Several things happened. One, which surprised Roosevelt because he was banking on his popularity, was that the public came out overwhelmingly against his stacking the Court. In many ways, it's a good sign because it shows what the American people can do when they act in a concerted manner. And no President has even suggested stacking the Court since then.

"But, on a darker note, several of the justices, instead of standing their ground, retracted or changed their votes on key issues."

"He intimidated the Court," Dave said.

"Yes, and the Court has been rather compliant with the wishes of the President and Congress ever since."

"Was the Court mostly Republican?" I asked.

"Seven of the nine justices had been appointed by Republicans."

"Then maybe he was right in wanting to add more justices to the Court," I said.

"Yes, maybe he was." Suddenly, he yawned very deeply. "And maybe the next time one or the other of the political parties controls the House, the Senate, and the White House, if the Supreme Court overrules anything they do, they can just appoint more judges so the vote goes their way. And if one party has enough members in the House and Senate and they don't want a President in the other party, they can impeach him. And..."

"I see what you're saying," Dave said. "In a round-about way you're saying 'If you're going to force things through by politically manipulating the system, then what's the point in having a system of checks and balances?'"

"That's what I was hoping you'd conclude," Mac responded.

"And if you start concentrating too much of the power in any one branch of the government, a system of checks and balances can't work," Dave added.

Mac yawned again. "That's right."

"But why did Roosevelt choose intimidation?" Dave asked.

"Perhaps he really believed his legislation could end the Depression. Or maybe he saw the truth, that what he had done so far wasn't working and he was getting desperate. But, whatever it was, he was at the height of his popularity and believed he could do pretty much anything he wanted. Intimidating the court was one of those things."

"How could he have been so popular," I asked, "if the Depression was dragging on, as you say?"

"I think that's a long story that includes a desperate population, a bad economy, the illusion that bad political action is better than no action at all, and ultimately a world war.

"But keep in mind that the Depression had spread around the world and strong leaders were wildly popular almost everywhere. It was a time when Hitler had risen to his heights in Germany, as had Mussolini in Italy, and both were as popular in their countries as FDR was here. Yet the Depression continued there, too. So maybe it shouldn't be a surprise that Roosevelt was riding the crest of his wave of popularity, though there were no improvements evident in the country."

Dave tapped his desk. "This isn't about the Depression," I want to hear more about the dangers of *Executive Orders*," he said.

Mac yawned again. "Just a second," he said, and he closed his eyes. "I love this chair," he added.

"It's the one we all sleep in," Dave said.

"Anyway, no other President wielded *Executive Orders*, or acted the part of the autocrat, as much as FDR did. As I said, in the end, little if anything he did helped end the Depression. But what he did do was entrench the power of *Executive Orders* and weaken the constitutional restraints our Founding Fathers had wisely placed on the presidency."

He put his head back again and closed his eyes.

Dave said, "You said something about Roosevelt signing the most infamous *Order* until John Kennedy took office. What *Orders* did Kennedy sign."

"We've got to talk about Truman, first." He still had his eyes closed.

"What do you mean we have to talk about Truman."

"Harry Truman had his run-ins with the Supreme Court, too, and it looked as though the Court may finally stand up to the Presidents and their *Executive Orders*."

He still had his eyes closed and we waited. And we waited.

...then, Mac fell asleep again.

"Is he asleep?" Dave asked.

I stood up at my desk so I could see clearly over my monitor. "Yes," I said.

"Wake him up," he whispered.

"No, you wake him up."

I looked at Dave. He looked at me. We were going to have to wait for Mac to finish his story on *Executive Orders*. Δ

Part V

How "emergency powers" and Executive Orders have turned America into a dictatorship in limbo

few hours earlier in the day Dave, Mac, and I were here at the office discussing *Executive Orders* as issued by various Presidents. The conversation was cut short when Mac, who had been leading the discussion, fell asleep in the stuffed chair we keep here. Dave, of course, is Dave Duffy, the fellow who publishes this magazine, and Mac is O.E. MacDougal, our poker playing friend from southern California.

Now that Mac was sleeping, Dave and I were taking care of business. It was almost 2:00 in the afternoon when, suddenly, there was a stirring followed by a low moan. I raised myself out of my seat and looked over my monitor. I saw Mac, his eyes still closed, trying to shift his position in the stuffed chair. His eyes opened a little, but just for a moment. Then they closed again.

"Oh," he said as he managed to shift his body a little. I settled back into my seat and figured he'd gone back to sleep.

I looked across the office at Dave who had a clear view of him. Dave was still watching him.

"Are you awake?" Dave asked.

"Yes, unfortunately I am," I heard Mac say and I rolled my chair to my right so I could see him around the monitor.

"In certain Third World countries," Mac said, "they use chairs like this to extract confessions. How can it have been so comfortable when I fell asleep a little while ago, and now I feel like I'm on the rack."

"It's hard to move around in that chair," Dave said, "and you become uncomfortable because you're stuck in just one position."

"I know," Mac said. "But why did I have to find it out the hard way."

"What about Kennedy?" Dave asked.

Mac raised an eyebrow. "What about him?" he asked.

"Before you went to sleep, you said Roosevelt signed the most infamous *Executive Order* until John Kennedy took office. What *Order* did he sign?"

"I also said we have to talk about Truman first. To understand how Kennedy's *Orders*—there was more than one—and the ones issued by subsequent Presidents have become a danger to us, you've got to understand what led up to them. You also have to understand what makes an *Executive Order* illegal and what constitutes a legal one. If you understand this you may also realize how we can effect a solution to this part of the potential dictatorship problem we now face in this country."

"Then where do we start?" Dave asked. "Do we have to go all the way back to George Washington again?"

"No, we just go back to Woodrow Wilson, fast-forward to Franklin Delano Roosevelt, then go on to Harry Truman."

"Okay, explain how Wilson figures into this stuff," Dave said.

Mac stood up and walked around the office as he stretched. Then he returned to the chair and flopped back into it.

Wilson's war powers

He began, "First, you've got to know that prior to our involvement in World War I, Wilson managed to steer through Congress a law called the *Trading with the Enemy Act* of 1917. The law must have seemed like a good idea at the time given that the biggest war civilization had seen, up to that point, was raging in Europe and it looked as though Wilson thought we should be in it.

"That act allowed the federal government to control certain commercial and monetary transactions within the borders of the United States. It was written to affect only those who would be defined or designated as enemies of the United States in time of war, and it pertained only to activities wholly involving transactions with those enemies. The act didn't pertain to ordinary American citizens, like you or me.

"Second, as I had said earlier this morning, Wilson was the first President to declare a national emergency and the first to bypass Congress and create government agencies without consulting with Congress, through the use of *Executive Orders*.

"He also used his considerable powers to suppress free speech and had people who spoke out about how his Administration had involved us in the war thrown into jail.

"But, what's important to what we're discussing is that the war ended—we won, by the way—and, when his Administration ended, Congress repealed most of the laws by which he had assumed the power of a potentate. But one of the laws not repealed was the *Trading with the Enemy Act*. There didn't seem to be any reason to repeal it. It didn't involve the American people, just those foreigners defined as enemies."

"Why did they have to repeal the other laws?" I asked.

"Not everyone was happy with the way Wilson had assumed almost dictatorial power during the war. Charles Evans Hughes, who at one time or another was an Associate Justice of the Supreme Court, Secretary of State, and finally the Chief Justice of the Supreme Court, wondered whether our constitutional form of government, having been suspended and subverted by the unconstitutional war powers acts Wilson had employed, could survive another 'emergency' of any kind.

"But not a lot of people listened to what Hughes, as well as many others, had to say concerning Wilson's abuse of the power of the presidency, because no emergency appeared to be on the horizon. It seemed as though all Wilson's wartime legislation was in the past and the United States entered the Roaring 20s and, other than a short post-war recession, a period of peace and financial prosperity ensued. It was, in fact, the most prosperous decade the U.S. had had in its history, up to that time."

"What were people like Hughes worried about?" Dave asked.

"Their concern was that not only do laws that create war powers go on and on, but like every other bureaucratic organization, the bureaucracies set up to administer the emergency powers don't go away and bureaucrats have to exercise their powers to justify their existence. Still, it seemed as though all was well with the United States.

The Depression begins

"Then, in 1929, the United States was shaken when the stock market crashed and this country, along with the rest of the world, slipped into the Great Depression.

"Herbert Hoover, the President at the beginning of the Depression, spent most of his Administration tinkering with the economy, hoping to end it, but he got nowhere. The Depression deepened and there seemed to be no way out of it. More and more people were put out of work until 25 percent of the American work force was unemployed. Then, in 1932, Franklin Delano Roosevelt was elected and a curious thing happened.

"As I had said earlier today, in the inaugural address he delivered for his first term, FDR first praised the legislative-executive balance of power our government enjoys, but in the next breath threatened to ignore it, darkly hinting that he would assume dictatorial powers if Congress opposed the course of action he was about to take. The programs he was proposing to end the Depression were a surprise to the American people, including Congress, because they were contrary to the policies he'd promised he'd institute during his campaign for office. And what's funny is that his campaign promises would probably have ended the Depression had he carried them out. But he took another route. He introduced socialistic solutions, and instead of the Depression ending, it hung on for another eight years until, thanks to World War II, we went into a wartime economy."

"But Roosevelt has always been credited with ending the Great Depression," I said.

"I know. You said that earlier today. But, as I pointed out, Roosevelt didn't end the Depression. He never served even one minute in office over anything but either a depressed economy or a wartime economy."

"So, what course of action did he take?" Dave asked.

"Upon taking office, Roosevelt decided to manage the entire economy. He closed the banks, made the personal possession of gold illegal, and began creating agencies to regulate all aspects of the economy. He acted without the consent of Congress and claimed his power stemmed from Wilson's *Trading with the Enemy Act* of 1917. This was the very same *Act* Wilson had created, before World War I, to seize German businesses."

"But you said that that act didn't pertain to the American people," Dave said.

"Roosevelt knew that. So, a few days after his inauguration, he convened Congress and, by a voice vote, the *Trading with the Enemy Act* of 1917 was amended to his satisfaction and the offending provisions were revised."

"Meaning...? Dave asked expectantly.

"That now, in accordance with the *Act*, during *any* emergency declared by the President, the *Trading with the Enemy Act* could be invoked, that he could create policy without consulting Congress, and that foreign powers weren't the only people subject to the *Act*. American citizens were, too."

The following is a list of *Executive Orders* signed by John Kennedy and is accompanied by a summary of what the EO says. Issued at the height of the Cold War, each contains the event of war as one of the reasons under which it could be activated. But each is also carefully worded so that the EO can take effect for any emergency declared by any President, and without the consent of either the people, the Congress, or the Courts. Each is written in accordance with the *War Powers Act*, but war is not a necessary condition for enacting them.

EO 10990; gives the government, (and since 1976, FEMA) the power to takeover all modes of transportation, control of highways, seaports etc.

EO 10995; allows the takeover of the communications media. (This means, of course, that even if Tom Brokow, Time Magazine, or the L.A. Times wants to question any takeover, if one happens, such questioning can be declared illegal. Why the media doesn't question this is beyond me.)

EO 10997; provides for the takeover of all electric, power, petroleum, gas, fuels, and minerals regardless of whether they are publicly or privately owned..

EO 10998; provides for the takeover of food resources and farms including farm equipment.

EO 11000; provides for mobilization of all civilians into work brigades under the government's supervision.

EO 11001; provides for government takeover of all health, education, and welfare functions, both public and private.

EO 11002; designates the Postmaster General to operate a national registration of all persons.

EO 11003; provides for the government to takeover all airports and aircraft.

EO 11004; provides for the Housing and Finance Authority to relocate communities, designate areas to be abandoned, and establish new locations for populations.

EO 11005; provides for the government to take over railroads, inland waterways, and public storage facilitiesMany of these EOs have been amended since they were first issued to make them broader or more encompassing, and some have been consolidated with other EOs. None, however, have been abandoned and none have been rewritten to narrow their scope or limit when they can be invoked.

"You're saying that Roosevelt now made it so that everyone fell under the jurisdiction of what was essentially a war powers act and that it applied to anything he deemed an emergency, not just war?" Dave asked.

"Yes, *any* emergency, and everybody was subject to it."

"And the Depression was an emergency," Dave said.

Mac nodded. "Remember," he said, "because it's important: with this new law, Roosevelt was able to declare emergencies and no longer had to consult with Congress when enacting his policies."

I nodded. Dave just waited for him to continue.

"Now," Mac said, "we can talk about Harry Truman and you'll see what came to make the difference between a legal and an illegal *Executive Order*.

"Truman, like FDR, used *Executive Orders* to advance his policies. Among other things that he attempted to do with them was to seize private property. Specifically, he attempted to nationalize the railroads in order to settle a strike. However, at this point the Supreme Court stepped in and ruled against that *Order*. Their reason for voiding the *Order*, the Court ruled, was that Truman had thrown the supposed system of checks and balances out of whack. They said he had overstepped his bounds by trying to create laws—namely, nationalizing an industry—when in fact, it is Congress' job to create laws.

"Now, they didn't rule that *Executive Orders* in general are illegal, because they're not. They just ruled that this one was not. What they said was that for an *Executive Order* to be valid it must either stem from the *Constitution* itself or from an act of Congress. And Truman hadn't based his takeover of the railroads on either the *Constitution* or on a law passed by Congress.

"Part of the ruling also stated that the President's job is to see that laws are faithfully executed, further refuting that he is the source of those laws or the lawmaker, himself.

"Now, along with remembering the *Trading with the Enemy Act*, you've got to remember what constitutes a legal *Executive Order*, because that's going to have an impact on what comes later."

"Because the *Trading with the Enemy Act* is now an act of Congress," Dave said. "And if a President bases his *Orders* on acts of Congress, which includes the *Trading with the Enemy Act*, then they're legal."

Mac tossed his hands in the air. "That's exactly right," he said. "*Executive Orders*, issued under any *emergency* declared by the President are now legal if they use the amended version of the *Trading with the Enemy Act* as their basis.

"For the remainder of his presidency, Truman issued plenty of *Executive Orders*, as has been the wont of all 20th century Presidents. And when Eisenhower sat in the White House, he too issued plenty of *Executive Orders*.

Kennedy's EOs

"Where it gets interesting is with the presidency of John Kennedy. During his short tenure in the White House, the United States and the Soviet Union began the arms race in earnest. In a few years each country had literally thousands of nuclear bombs pointed at the other and the threat of nuclear war seemed very real.

"The question arose: how would we survive as a society if a nuclear war started? How would such a war be conducted? Unlike World War II where battles could be fought over days and movements of troops and supplies could be conducted over months, the nuclear war that would be World War III would require lightning-fast decisions.

"To deal with this problem, Kennedy went on an *Executive Order* writing spree the likes of which this country never before saw. The *Orders* he wrote granted him, and subsequent Presidents, dictatorial powers, but not just in the event of a nuclear war. He also included any other emergency declared by the President. Go look on a government website and see what *Orders* he put in place. They're available for anyone to read. And those *Orders*, or their amended later versions, are still on the books."

"What do they cover?" I asked.

"They cover a multitude of things, from government control of transportation to communications. They include control of power, food, health—virtually every aspect of our lives. And, as I said, they don't say 'only in the case of a nuclear war.' And though the intent may have been honorable, the potential for abuse is considerable. And during any of these crises, the *Constitution* is up in the air.

"Naturally, none of these *Orders* were voted on by Congress or by the electorate."

"But wouldn't *Executive Orders* that suspend the *Constitution* be ruled unconstitutional?" Dave asked.

"Suspension of the *Constitution* is allowed by the *Constitution*."

"You're kidding," Dave said.

I almost fell out of my chair.

"No, I'm not. *Article I, Section 9* of the *Constitution* and the *5th Amendment* both state that we cannot be arrested, tried, or convicted, *unless* we're in the middle of a rebellion, being invaded, or for other reasons of *public safety*. In other words, the *Constitution* could be suspended but only in the event of dire emergency. What 20th century politicians have done is create the concept of perpetual emergency. Under any ongoing emergency we have in this country, the government can do anything it wants and the *Constitution* has only been in effect at the pleasure of the President since 1933."

"Why doesn't Congress or the Supreme Court just call an end to the emergency powers?"

"They can't. Part of the Act of 1933 said the emergency was in effect until the President declared it was over. Counting Roosevelt as the first, we've had 12 successive Presidents, none of whom have seen fit to end the emergency and, therefore, all of them can issue *Executive Orders* that would seem contrary to the *Constitution*. Furthermore, the *Constitution* has been null and void any time any President has declared emergency powers since March 9, 1933. That's almost 70 years if anyone is doing the math."

"Then Kennedy's *Orders*..." Dave began.

"...and those in the same vein that have been passed by other Presidents..." Mac interrupted.

"...would appear to be a *real* threat," Dave said. "Do you think they would ever really be used for anything other than our survival during an all-out war?"

"The answer to your question is that no one knows. But it was by allowing one man to aggrandize so much awesome power that the Germans gave themselves Hitler. At some future date we may be faced with the same kind of leader—and then again, we may not. We're not mandating a Hitler, but why a country that was founded on individual freedoms would want to clear the way for one is beyond me."

"Have any Presidents issued any similar *Orders* since Kennedy issued his?" Dave asked.

"The *Executive Orders* that sit silently, waiting for a President to declare the ultimate emergency, have been amended and consolidated and most have now come under the purview of FEMA, the Federal Emergency Management Agency. FEMA itself was created by *Executive Order* by Jimmy Carter, though similar, weaker agencies existed before it, including Nixon's Federal Emergency Preparedness Agency, the forerunner of FEMA.

"Since Kennedy, Presidents have enhanced FEMA's powers so that during any emergency declared by the President it has the power to take control of all transportation; take over all electric, power, petroleum, gas, fuels, and mining; take over radio and television; take over food production including farms; mobilize any and all civilians into work brigades to be supervised by the government; take over health, education, and welfare; order the registration of all persons in the United States; and to relocate communities and any population groups as directed.

"None of this has been authorized, approved, or directed by Congress. The American people neither provide nor are they even allowed to provide input. There is no public debate.

"And last, it has the power to suspend the *Constitution*, if it deems it necessary."

"It's hard to believe this could happen," Dave said.

Mac said, "If there is a dictatorship imposed, the *Constitution* will not be amended. It will remain in place, but it will be void because of the ongoing 'national emergency' that will never end. Our *Constitution* will continue to be a showcase to the world, a demonstration of how men can govern themselves if they want to protect their rights. But it will not be in force. It will be dead.

"And that brings us to where we are today," Mac said. "Maybe it will never be acted upon. Perhaps, for the first time in history, as far as I know, the mechanisms for tyranny will be set in place but never be acted upon.

"Though the American people believe they have a constitutional democratic republic, what we really have are a mass of laws waiting silently for some President, for whatever the reason, to legally pull the trigger that will suspend the *Constitution* and legally make the man in the White House the only law of the land."

"But no President since FDR has threatened to act as dictator," I said.

"Just a few years ago," Mac said, "when the Republican-controlled Congress and President Clinton were at loggerheads over some piece of legislation, Clinton hinted that, if the Congress didn't come around he would bypass them and enact the laws he wanted through *Executive Orders*. The media loved this threat to the Republicans, but none of them pointed out that Congress is supposed to be expressing the will of the people and enacting the laws of the land and that, if Clinton can bypass the Congress, he was, in fact, acting as dictator.

"Now, as it turned out, he didn't carry out his threat, but his message was clear: by simply declaring an emergency the President can enact

---

Amendment V

No person shall be held to answer for a capital, or otherwise infamous crime, unless on a presentment or indictment of a Grand Jury, *except in cases arising in the land or naval forces, or in the Militia, when in actual service in time of War or public danger;...*

101

any laws he wants and democracy, the Congress, the people, and the *Constitution* including the *Bill of Rights* be damned.

"Now, it may be that no President will ever act as a dictator, but why do we want to make that kind of power available?

"I believe, if most people were asked if they wanted this much power vested in any President, they'd say no. Yet the Congress, the people, and in particular, the mass media have ignored them and let it happen. We now have a dictatorship waiting to *legally* happen. We have a dictatorship in limbo. Maybe it will never happen. But letting these *Orders* stand is the equivalent of leaving a loaded gun on the kitchen table with a houseful of kids. Why would you do that, even if you felt like you could trust *most* of them?"

"Why doesn't the Congress or the Supreme Court just end these emergencies themselves?" I asked.

"They can't. The original emergency powers Roosevelt assumed as President are still in effect. In September of 1976 Congress considered, then failed, to end them. It wasn't that they refused to, they simply found out that they couldn't. By law, ending the emergency requires that the President declare that the emergency is over. No President since Roosevelt has felt compelled to do so.

"In fact, under the current law, any emergency declared by the President under the *Trading with the Enemy Act* continues until he himself declares it is over.

"The truth is that the overwhelming majority of people in the United States have lived under this quasi-dictatorship we now have in this country. They don't know any different. They think this is the way the country is supposed to be run. They don't realize that any time the President wants, he can declare an emergency and ignore the *Constitution*."

"So we could fall into a dictatorship of endless emergencies," Dave said.

"Yes. In his novel, *Nineteen Eighty-four*, George Orwell describes how the main character, Winston Smith, realizes that the country he lives in is under a perpetual dictatorship because there is a perpetual state of emergency, a perpetual state of war.

"That's where America seems to be headed today."

"Why don't people know this?" I asked.

"It's not something that's taught in high school civics, and I've sat in on political science classes in college and, as far as I can tell, it's never mentioned there."

"Why aren't newscasters talking about it?" I asked.

"Why would they? Television newscasters aren't journalists; they're celebrities who read what's put in front of them. And the few journalists who do point it out suffer *ad hominem* attacks in which their character is attacked and the issue itself is ignored."

The solution

"Is there a solution?" Dave asked.

"Of course there is," Mac said. "In fact, of all the things that make a dictatorship possible in this country, this is the one that could be most readily solved. But I don't think it's going to happen."

"What's the solution?" Dave asked.

"The first step would be to start making government by emergency a campaign issue in the next presidential election, and every presidential election until this government by emergency edicts is abolished. Make it a litmus test for the presidency.

"Of course, before it can become a campaign issue, the major media outlets are going to have to inform the public. I don't think it's going to happen."

"Why?" Dave asked.

"Because most of them are unaware of it, and as the media is largely liberal, government by decree was initiated by one of their own and they're not going to want to undo anything promulgated by one of their own.

"But a 30-minute segment on *60 Minutes* and cover articles by *Time*, *Newsweek*, and other large circulation news magazines would go miles toward exposing to the American public that we are no longer truly a democratic constitutional republic."

"The second step would be for Congress to repeal Title 12 USC 95(a) and 95(b). These are the amendments to the *Trading with the Enemy Act* by which Congress vested so much power in the President.

"The third thing we should do is take past *Executive Orders* that have been vaguely written so they cover virtually anything the President deems to be an emergency, and specify the emergencies those *Executive Orders* can cover and place a time limit for which they can be in effect. The way Kennedy's *Executive Orders* were sold to the public—what public that actually listened—was that they were needed in the event of nuclear war. So limit them to nuclear war. Would that be too difficult?"

"And if the the *Executive Order* is required for an emergency, it should be an emergency with a sunset date or with the words, 'until Congress can convene to consider the matter,' or some other such phrase?"

"Is that it on the dangers of *Executive Orders*?" Dave asked.

"We could go on, but this more or less sums the dangers up."

"You said you thought there were dangers from the creation of the new professional Army we now have."

"Except it isn't so new anymore," Mac said.

"What do you have to say about that?" I asked. "I think the concept of a professional Army is great."

Mac got out of the chair again. "I can't talk about this stuff on an empty stomach. Let's get out of here and find some lunch."

"All you do is sleep and eat," Dave said.

"Is that a problem?" Mac asked as we walked out the door. Δ

Part VI

How judges and prosecutors have undermined the right of the American people to nullify laws

It was mid-afternoon and, with Mac awake again, Dave suggested we take a ride. So he, Mac, and I left the office and went to get a late lunch at a little fish and chips restaurant down the coast in the town of Brookings. Dave was killing two birds with one stone with this trip because he also had to pick up some computer supplies.

Dave, of course, is Dave Duffy, the publisher of this magazine, and Mac is O.E, MacDougal, our poker-playing friend from southern California. We'd spent most of the morning talking about what Mac calls "the Coming American Dictatorship." Apparently, what concerns him is not so much some Hitler or Stalin-like figure suddenly leaping out of the woodwork and assuming power; it's the continuing erosion of our rights, as government at all levels grows and becomes more intrusive in our lives. He's especially concerned about the loss of rights which has accompanied the explosive growth of government in this country since 1933.

As we reached Dave's car, Mac indicated I should get in the passenger's seat in front while he climbed in back. I did.

After we were all belted in Dave asked, "Mac, what do you think is the most important thing people should do to protect their rights?"

"Get out the vote and throw the bums who are in there out of office," I said.

"That would help," Mac said. "If the American people had all along made it clear to our elected officials, at the polling booth, that we wouldn't tolerate infringements of our freedoms, we wouldn't have the endless succession of laws that make one exception to our rights after another.

"And we wouldn't have these new rights invented by Congress, the White House, and various bureaucrats that create privileges for one segment of society but mandate that other segment of society *must* provide those privileges, whether those privileged parts of society are corporations or people on welfare.

"We'd also have control over those bureaucracies that have been spawned and which seem to rule us now. In fact, the bureaucracies would be vastly smaller and there'd be fewer of them, and most of the people who currently have government jobs or jobs in private industry that support government bureaucracies would have to go out and get productive jobs, and that would benefit us all."

Jury trials

"I get the impression," Dave said, "that you feel there's something other than the voting that would change things."

"There is at least one."

"And that is...?" Dave asked.

"If Americans would pay more attention to what goes on in courtrooms, and particularly pay attention to the way government, at all levels, stacks juries and has made them pawns of the government. If we would stop that, it would put us in a position to get control over abusive government."

"How would we make that happen? How would we get Americans more aware of what's going on in courtrooms?" Dave asked.

"Two things would have to happen. First, we'd have to insist that jurors be made aware of their real power in the courtroom. Second, we'd have to insist on more jury trials."

"More jury trials?" Dave asked.

"Yes, we should demand that anytime a citizen is in a position to lose his personal property, his freedom, or his life, that he or she should be able to demand and receive a trial before a *random* jury of his peers."

"This is something we've talked about before," Dave said.

"Yes, it is," Mac said.

"Could we talk about it, again?" I asked. "Especially what you just said—'a *random* jury of our peers.'"

"Sure. But first we've got to understand the two issues here. The **first** concerns what citizens should know when they sit on a jury. The **second** is that there are more and more 'crimes' of which you can be accused, for which you may fined, have your property seized, be imprisoned, or even executed—but for which you will not receive a jury trial.

"We should insist that if the government wants to try you, it should do so before a jury of citizens who are the final arbiters of whether or not you have really committed a crime."

"What's wrong with trials before a judge?" I asked.

"Nothing—if that's what *you* want when you're the defendant. But unless you request a trial before a judge, you should be able to exercise the option of being tried before your fellow citizens."

"Why are jury trials so important?" I asked.

"The laws are there to control how we act in certain circumstances. We're supposed to obey them. So we, the citizens, should insist that the laws make sense and that they're applied fairly. And when we sit on juries, we should not only hear the government's case against one of *us*, but ensure the laws are just.

"This isn't something I just thought up," he added. "The demand for jury trials, where the juries are made up of a group of the defendant's peers—and in this country, that would be our fellow citizens—goes all the way back to the *Magna Carta*, because even then jury trials were meant to stop government abuse."

"But you say we don't always get jury trials," Dave said. "When aren't jury trials used?"

"It isn't just a question of when they aren't used, it's a question of when they aren't even *allowed*. Among the cases in which they aren't allowed are IRS cases, family law cases, and in many federal courts."

"But tax law is very difficult to understand," I said, taking the side of the government in this case. "Juries may not be able to understand the complexities and ramifications of such cases."

"Think about what that means. You're saying that tax law is too difficult for the average juror to understand after several days of testimony in a court case—after it's been explained to him by experts. Yet, the average Joe on the street still has to abide by those laws. How can laws that can deprive us of our property and our freedom be fair if jurors can't even understand them when they're explained in a courtroom? Those are some of the kinds of laws that fully informed juries, that is, juries who know their rights, would refuse to convict under.

"What I would like to see done is to let jurors hear those cases and any other cases where the government has brought suit against a citizen. And if the laws are too confusing, the jury can be the first to tell the government, 'Screw you.' The result would be that in a short time politicians and bureaucrats would know what laws the American people will and won't tolerate."

"So you're saying that if we insisted that more trials be presented before juries we'd have better laws," Dave said.

"Yes. If the American people really want fair and sensible laws, they're going to have to see how they're applied, firsthand. I say let juries made up of the citizenry—made up of average citizens—hear *all* the cases.

"But coupled with that, of course, the jurors must be informed of their right to jury nullification. Then I can guarantee you that the only laws that will be left will be sensible laws."

"This sounds like it's too simple of a solution," Dave said. "Yet, on the surface it seems that this is one thing that could stop runaway government."

"Sure, but government at all levels has succeeded in denying juries their powers, and often succeeded just denying us jury trials. They have managed to get the governed—that's us, the average citizens—out of the loop. But what makes it worse is that we, the average citizens, don't care that we've been taken out of the loop. We don't care what laws are being passed and how bad laws, laws that infringe upon our rights, are applied—against us."

"But we can change bad laws at the ballot box," I said. "We can elect different people to get rid of bad laws and pass better laws."

"We can, but that takes years. First you've got to elect a majority who agree on making a fair law, then you have to overcome the resistance to changes because of so-called special interests who want the law in place, and then you've got to hope that the changes are sensible.

"Keep in mind that when you expect people to vote to change bad laws you're assuming that the voters are seeing the bad laws in action. But the fact is only a small percentage of the citizenry actually see the laws applied. And those who do are often limited to the defendant and 12 jurors. You can't expect major changes in the law when you depend on the entire of the electorate to see each and every law.

"The other problem is what happens to the accused while we're waiting years, even decades, for the electorate to change the state legislatures or the Congress so that the laws are changed?

"In the early part of the 20th century, when Prohibition was part of the law of the land, the attempts to repeal it were taking years. Meanwhile, peoples' lives were being ruined.

"However, juries began showing their unwillingness to convict people in courtrooms under those laws and prosecutors became increasingly reluctant to prosecute these cases.

"Jury by jury, the American people were sending a message to the government that they wouldn't tolerate laws *that were bad*."

"Well, I know I'd hate to have my life ruined by bad laws and have to sit in some stinking cell waiting for some guy watching reruns of *My Favorite Martian* to get off his duff and vote for something sensible," Dave said.

I slumped back in my seat trying to think of how to respond to this.

"The voting booth is fine," Mac said. "But what we actually need is democracy in *both* the ballot box *and* the jury box."

"What if you had to choose only one?" Dave asked, and I got the feeling he was asking it to be funny.

We passed Cape Sebastian, the highest point on the Oregon coast, and started down the hill.

Mac said, "If I had to pick just one, I'd rather have democracy in the jury box than at the ballot box."

"Really?" Dave asked. "Why?"

"At the ballot box millions of people go to vote who don't know what the issues are. That's part of the reason why we have so many bad laws. However, in the jury box, it doesn't matter what you've been doing up until the moment you sit there. You can't help but hear what the issues really are. At least the ones that relate to the case at hand. I think people leave the jury box better informed than when they got there. I think they make better decisions in the jury box than they do in the ballot box.

"On the other hand, at the ballot box people are stupid when they show up and stupid when they leave."

He paused. "But, in reality, we can't have one without the other. Unfortunately, whereas as voters we often understand the power of the ballot, when we're jurors we usually don't know that while we are sitting in the jury box we are the most powerful force in the courtroom.

We are more powerful than the judge or any of the attorneys there. We are trying not only the defendant, but we also have an opportunity to try the law."

"And when a jury finds *against the law*, that's jury nullification," Dave said.

"That's right," Mac responded.

"Jury nullification?" I asked.

"We've talked about it before," Dave said.

I nodded as I began to remember a little about it.

Mac went on, "Jury nullification is when a jury acquits a person of a crime, even though it's clear he committed the crime, because the jurors feel there are extenuating circumstances, or because they feel the law is unjust, or because the sentence will be too harsh, or because they feel the law is applied unfairly."

I looked over the backseat and asked, "But shouldn't we just let the legislators change these things? I don't think it's the jury's place to change the law."

"There are two things wrong with that," he replied. "The first is that the jury isn't changing the law. They're just refusing to apply it in a particular case. However, I think it's clear that if prosecutors can't win cases under a particular law, because one jury after another refuses to apply it, they will stop using that law to prosecute the citizens, and the legislature will get the message. On the other hand, continuing to convict, even when you know the law is wrong, sends the wrong message to both the prosecutors and the legislature. It's saying that we the citizens feel the law is okay.

"The second thing wrong with that scenario—and this is crucial to stopping abuses by the state—is that even if a judge tells me I have to, I'm not going to ruin a fellow citizen's life while the legislature spends years pondering whether to change it or not. Particularly when so many of our laws have been passed, not because they are sensible, but because they appease one special interest group or another.

"I'm not going to act like a guard at a concentration camp and just 'follow orders,'" he said. "If the law is wrong, it's wrong."

No one said anything for a moment.

"Do you have examples of each of the things you just mentioned?" Dave asked Mac. "You know, nullifying laws because of extenuating circumstances, because laws are unjust, sentences that are too harsh, or a law is unfairly applied?"

"Sure. In the first case, imagine a man is called to his daughter's home because her boyfriend has threatened to come back and kill her. He gets to his daughter's house and she has a gun to protect herself. The boyfriend arrives, still threatening to kill her *and her father*, and he breaks down the door. The woman's father takes the gun and kills the boyfriend. It would appear to be a case of self defense. But it turns out the father is an ex-felon and, by law, is not allowed to handle a gun.

"So, even though he used the gun in self defense, and even though it's clear that he saved his daughter's life, as well as his own, the D.A. has him arrested for violating that gun law.

"In just such a case, which happened some years back in Georgia, the jury was instructed to bring a verdict of 'guilty' if the prosecution proved its case. And there was no question that the prosecution had proved its case. Unaware that they could have refused to bring a guilty verdict because of extenuating circumstances, the jury followed the judge's explicit instructions and rendered the only verdict they thought possible: guilty.

"After the trial, several of the jurors even approached the defendant and told him—some crying—that none of them wanted to bring a guilty verdict, but that they felt 'ordered' to obey the judge.

"Only later did they find out that they didn't have to. But now the guy is serving time.

"But had just one of those jurors the courage to defy the judge's faulty instructions, or had just one of them known what his or her real rights and duties as a juror were, the man may well have gone free."

"There should have been a mistrial because of faulty instructions to the jury," I said.

"You'd think so. But the Supreme Court has already ruled that a judge's failure to inform the jury of its right to nullification is not grounds for a mistrial. In fact, the Court has ruled that even if the judge denies that the right exists..."

"You mean 'lies to the jury,'" Dave interrupted.

"Yes," Mac said. "Even that is not grounds for a mistrial."

"Why didn't the defendant's lawyer tell the jury about jury nullification?" I asked.

"Because most judges would either find that lawyer in contempt of court, or he'd declare a mistrial and they'd have to start all over again.

"And, if you were wondering, the Supreme Court has also ruled that it's okay for judges to prevent lawyers from explaining nullification to juries."

We crossed over the Pistol River and I thought it was ironic, considering Mac's example, that we were doing so at that time.

"In the second case," Mac continued, "imagine a woman with cancer who is undergoing radiation and chemotherapy and finds the only way she can make it through the treatment, and the only way she can keep food down, is by smoking marijuana. Imagine also that her doctor is aware of this and has given her his approval."

"As I understand it, the marijuana actually helps during those treatments," Dave said.

"That's the way I understand it, too," Mac said. Then he continued. "Now, say smoking marijuana is illegal where she lives and she's caught and brought to trial, and you're on the jury. The prosecution proves she was smoking. She, in fact, admits she was smoking. Even her doctor testifies that he knew she was smoking, but he says it was helping her.

"But, we are told by the prosecution that the question of marijuana's medical benefits are of no concern to the jury in the case. And you're on the jury. The judge instructs you to bring a verdict of guilty if the prosecution has proved its case. And it has proved its case. What's your verdict?"

"Well," I said, "now I know I don't have to bring a verdict of guilty, so I wouldn't."

"But in similar trials, a lot of juries do," he said.

"This would then be another case where an informed jury would throw the state's case out," Dave said.

"That's right," Mac replied.

"What's an example of an unjust sentence?" Dave asked.

"Take as an example the 'three strikes' laws. Various states have passed them. When the legislators were campaigning for them, they led the citizens to believe that they were going to be used to put 'career criminals' away forever. But in one of the first cases in California, a man with two felony convictions against him was being tried under the three strikes law for walking out of a Taco Bell without paying. He was, technically, shoplifting, but the state was making it a felony case and, if convicted, the man was going to spend the rest of his life behind bars. Now, if I knew more of the history of this man perhaps I'd agree he should die behind bars. But barring that, if his 'life of crime' was no more than stealing food when he was hungry, would you be willing to give him life imprisonment over three or four dollars worth of fast food?"

"I guess I wouldn't," I said.

"Then, either you'd hang the jury or convince them that this case was ridiculous and they should acquit the guy and send a message to the prosecutor.

"But in thousands of cases, juries unwillingly send people to jail for absurdly long sentences. In fact, they often do it because they don't even know what the sentence is going to be. It's one more of the things we should insist on when we're asked to pass judgment on our fellow man: what's the penalty if we convict him? In many cases, jurors have said they would never have voted for conviction if they'd known how harsh a penalty was going to be meted out."

"What about unfairly applied laws?" Dave asked.

"Do you remember about 25 years ago, when you were living in Oxnard, California, you were stopped by the police. You were in front of your house, drinking a beer on the sidewalk?"

"Yes."

"What did they tell you?"

"They said I couldn't drink on the street."

"And you asked, 'How come?' and the cop said...?"

"He said it was 'one of those laws we have to keep the Mexicans in line.'"

"As I recall, you were outraged by that statement. Here's a law that would seem to apply to everyone, but its real use was against Mexicans. Now, would you bring a verdict of guilty against a Mexican if you were on the jury in a case that was applied only to Mexicans?"

Dave shook his head and said, "No, of course not."

"Well, there you have it. Those were examples of cases where jury nullification would be applied," Mac said.

"And you say jury nullification goes all the way back to the Magna Carta," I said.

"In other cultures, it even predates that. But the whole purpose of ensuring jury trials was to ensure that, if the king—the government—managed to get unjust laws passed, the people still had the power to peacefully nullify them.

Rights and nullification

"Many of the rights we have today were recognized by the government only because of jury nullification."

"Like what?" Dave asked.

"The source of religious freedom in England, and hence the source of religious freedom in the English colonies, including the American colonies, can be traced back to 1670 and the refusal of a London jury to convict William Penn for preaching Quaker beliefs. But the court, outraged by the jury's verdict, imprisoned the jurors for a time and ordered them to change their verdict. But they wouldn't relent. Finally, another English judge ordered the jury's verdict to stand claiming that, unless a jurors' decision was coerced or suborned, a jury's verdict is beyond review. In effect, he was saying, what's the point in having a jury involved in a trial if the state is going to dictate the jury's verdict?

"Twenty-two years later, in Salem, Massachusetts, the witch trials ground to a halt because juries began refusing to return convictions, even though the defendants met all the requirements set out by the colonial government to be deemed guilty of witchcraft. There must have been fifty such acquittals before the colony gave up trying citizens as 'witches.'"

"What right did we get out of that?" I asked.

"Part of the reason the juries stopped returning guilty verdicts in the witch trials was because the defendants were frequently tortured to extract confessions. The juries didn't think confessions extracted under torture were reliable.

"This wasn't lost on the Founding Fathers of this country who, almost 100 years later, included the right against self-incrimination in the *Fifth Amendment*. The way the Founding Fathers said it was, '...nor be compelled in any criminal case to be a witness against himself...'

"The right to a free press was established in the North American colonies by a jury in 1735, before it was guaranteed by the *Bill of Rights* in 1791."

"What was that case?" Dave asked.

"John Zenger, a printer in New York, was arrested and tried for libel because he published attacks on the colonial governor. The government's case was based on a law that forbade attacks on the government, even if the allegations were true. Zenger's attorney, a Philadelphia lawyer named Andrew Hamilton, convinced the jury to acquit Zenger even though he was clearly in violation of the law.

**The Fully Informed Jury Association (FIJA)
proposes a constitutional amendment such as the following:**

Whenever government is one of the parties in a trial by jury, the court shall inform the jurors that each of them has an inherent right to vote on the verdict, in the direction of mercy, according to his own conscience and sense of justice. Exercise of this right may include jury consideration of the defendant's motives and circumstances, degree of harm done, and evaluation of the law itself. Failure to so inform the jury is grounds for mistrial and another trial by jury.

For more information go to **www.fija.org**

"In 1798, during the Administration of John Adams, the *Sedition Act* was passed to ban the publishing of writings against the government or the inciting of opposition to any act of Congress or the president."

"More censorship," Dave said.

"Yes, and when the government brought various publishers to trial, they soon found out it was almost impossible to get convictions, even though it was clear the publishers were in violation of the *Act*."

Dave said, "But the *First Amendment*, guaranteeing freedom of the press, was just..." He thought a second. "...the *Bill of Rights* was enacted in 1791...so it was just seven years old."

"That's right. And, of course, the jurors of that time would have been intimately familiar with their rights as well as their power to nullify bad laws. But if one of today's judges was overseeing one of those cases, he or she would have instructed the jurors to disregard the *First Amendment* and bring a verdict of guilty if the defendants were shown to be in violation of the *Sedition Act*."

"But the *Constitution* is the law of the land," Dave said. "It says so right in the *Constitution* itself."

"It does," Mac said. "But today's judges have convinced jurors that they are allowed to exclude it from *their* courtrooms."

"When do they ever do that?" I asked.

117

Mac shrugged. "In almost every courtroom in this country, if you are arrested on a weapons charge, you are not allowed to introduce the *Second Amendment* into your case."

"Even though it's the law of the land," Dave said flatly.

Mac nodded.

"But the *Constitution* is supposed to be the law that binds the government..." Dave said and his voice trailed off.

Mac nodded again.

"So, we're supposed to obey the laws they pass to the letter, but the one set of laws they are *obligated* to adhere to, the set that we're told hundreds of thousands of soldiers have died for..."

"Don't keep going on this," Mac said, "Or you'll get *me* started."

I looked back at Mac. "What other times has jury nullification made a difference?" I interrupted.

"Well, prior to the Civil War, the failure of the *Fugitive Slave Act*, as it was originally passed, came about because juries refused to return convictions."

"What was the *Fugitive Slave Act*?" I asked.

"It was a law, passed by Congress, that ordered the return of runaway slaves who had fled their masters in the South and took refuge in the North. There was an option in the *Act* allowing the slaves to ask for a jury trial. Of course, what happened was that it immediately became almost impossible to get a northern jury to find against the erstwhile slaves and order their return to a life of slavery in the South."

"Why didn't that end slavery?" I asked. "Why'd we wind up with the Civil War, anyway?"

"In part because the War wasn't over slavery, though slavery was a factor. It was actually about secession. But jury nullification in these cases couldn't have ended slavery, anyway, because the federal government's reaction was to circumvent the people and pass a law that ended jury trials in these cases."

"You mean, when the government couldn't get its way in court, it just ended jury trials?" Dave asked.

"That's exactly what it did. That's why the federal government today has so many trials without juries. It realizes that there are a great many cases, such as tax cases and cases involving bureaucratic decrees, where their cases would be thrown out one after another if juries, made up of private citizens, realized just how ludicrous many laws are."

"What other things have been changed in this country by jury nullification?" I asked.

"In the 20th century Prohibition ended because juries refused to convict people of the *consensual crime* of drinking booze. The *XXI Amendment*, which repealed Prohibition, was the direct result of those juries."

"So, it's fair to say that the government doesn't like jury nullification," Dave said. "They probably see it as though it's a kind of an 'in your face' response from the citizens."

"That's right. The state never likes it when the governed disagree with its laws. William Penn's trial wasn't the only time when jurors were fined, imprisoned, and even tortured for returning verdicts the state didn't like. There were times, before Penn's trial, when the jurors and even their families went to prison because the state didn't like the jury's decision."

"What do they do to jurors today when they refuse to convict defendants that the government thinks they should have?" Dave asked.

"In this country? Nothing. *Amendment VII* of the *Constitution* guarantees that jury verdicts which nullify laws cannot be reviewed and the Supreme Court has affirmed this. However, in a recent court case a Colorado woman named Laura Kriho was jailed for not telling the judge she understood jury nullification. She was eventually released, but the message has been sent to other jurors that they had best toe the line or pay for it.

"However, judges usually don't have to do anything that drastic, because today the government's strategy is to make sure that jurors who would question the law never get impanelled."

"What do you mean?" I asked as I turned back to see him again.

"Just what I said. The government now routinely excludes from a jury anyone who would question the law."

I thought about that for a few seconds. "Well, it may make sense," I said. "I'd be afraid that if juries weren't bound by the judges' instructions that we'd have anarchy."

"For the first 125 years of this country, juries were routinely instructed by trial judges that they could judge the law as well as the defendant. And, as I pointed out, there were many times when defendants were acquitted because the jurors found the laws unfair or unjust—even though the defendants were obviously guilty. But there are no references to anarchy in this country during that time. You don't know something I'm not aware of, do you?"

I didn't respond.

Nullification and the Founding Fathers

"Did the guys who gave us the *Constitution* believe jurors have the right to nullify laws?" Dave asked.

"You can find it in the writings of many of the Founding Fathers."

"Can you quote a few?" Dave asked.

Mac looked up at the roof of the car for a moment. "Thomas Jefferson, President and author of the *Declaration of Independence*, said, 'I consider trial by jury as the only anchor ever yet imagined by man, by which a government can be held to the principles of its constitution.'

"John Adams, the second President, and also a signer of the *Declaration of Independence*, wrote, 'It is not only his right, but his duty'—meaning the juror's right and duty—'to find the verdict according to his own best understanding, judgement, and conscience, though in direct opposition to the direction of the court.'

"Alexander Hamilton, the first Secretary of the Treasury, wrote, 'Jurors should acquit, even against the judge's instruction…if exercising their judgement with discretion and honesty they have a clear conviction that the charge of the court is wrong.'"

"But none of these guys were judges," Dave said. "What did the legal eagles of their day have to say?"

"John Jay, the first Chief Justice of the Supreme Court, said, 'The jury has the right to judge both the law as well as the fact in controversy.'

"More recently, Chief Justice Oliver Wendell Holmes said, 'The jury has the power to bring a verdict in the teeth of both the law and the facts,' meaning, they could disregard both the law and the evidence if they thought it was necessary.

"Harlan Stone, Chief Justice from 1941 to 1946 said, 'If a juror feels that the statute involved in any criminal offense is unfair, or that it infringes upon the defendant's natural God-given unalienable, or constitutional rights, then it is his duty to affirm that the offending statute is really no law at all and that the violation of it is no crime at all—for no one is bound to obey an unjust law…the law itself is on trial, quite as much as the cause which is to be decided.'

"And, if you need something in your own lifetime, in 1972, the D.C. Court of Appeals ruled the jury has an '…unreviewable and irreversible power…to acquit in disregard of the instruction on the law given by the trial judge.'"

"In the defense of free speech, a free press, the right to bear arms, and many others causes, the world has become a better place to live because juries refused to convict the accused even though they had clearly broken the law.

"And in recent years juries have acquitted defendants who openly admitted violating laws they considered unjust. Homeschoolers, draft resisters, homosexuals, tax resisters, cancer patients who were arrested for marijuana use and possession, gun owners, and others who have had their rights trampled upon by our runaway government have managed to convince a jury that they were right and the government was wrong and the jury has acquitted them despite the fact that they had violated the law.

"If enough juries acquit defendants who have clearly violated a bad law, the State will eventually give up and quit trying to enforce that law."

"But you said the state now ensures that those who would question the law are not on juries."

"Yes, and that's something the American people have got to change."

"But aren't the courts, the Supreme Court in particular, really the ones who should determine what our rights are?" I asked.

"No. We have to hope that the courts will protect our rights, in accordance with the *Constitution*, but we should never lose sight of the fact that when we depend upon the courts, we are asking a *branch of the government* to interpret and make the determination what our rights are when those very rights are, in fact, *restraints against the government*."

"I never thought of it that way," Dave said.

"Freedom of speech, freedom of lawful assembly, and freedom of the press in the *First Amendment* are there so we can speak out against the government. The right to bear arms was intended primarily to counter government force. The guarantee of public trials, before juries of our peers, is there so that the government is not allowed to jail us, fine us, or execute us without our fellow citizens determining that it's the proper thing to do. In the end, we have to protect those rights ourselves. If we let the government be the final arbiter of our rights, then they are not rights at all; they're privileges.

"Furthermore, when we allow judges to instruct the jurors to bring verdicts of guilty, even when the law is wrong, he's trying to subvert the power of juries that was begun with the signing of the *Magna Carta* in 1215.

"Then who should interpret our rights?" I asked.

"The same people who have to die for them on battlefields," he said.

"You mean us," Dave said.

"But in this country, *the people are the government*," I countered.

"If that were true, the *Constitution* wouldn't be written the way it is," Mac said. "The Founding Fathers worded the *Constitution* the way they did because they were fully aware that the government and the people are not the same."

Solutions

We were nearing Brookings and Dave said, "Ever since you started talking with us about these issues, you've included possible solutions. How should we go about trying to get jury nullification back in the courts?"

"Well, first, there should be *no* special courts without juries when our rights are at stake. That is, no IRS courts, no family courts, or any other courts without juries. Randomly drawn juries, taken from the citizenry, should hear all of the cases and be the ones to determine guilt or innocence. And guilty verdicts should have to be unanimous."

"Having so many jury trials would clog up the court system," I said. "It's already clogged enough as it is."

"Well, the most obvious thing that should be done to unclog the court system is to stop prosecuting victimless or consensual crimes. That would automatically put an end to 80 percent of all trials."

"Not only that," Dave said, "I find it difficult to swallow that judges, prosecutors, and politicians think we should be divested of our rights because it's *inconvenient* for them. If the job's too hard for them, let them find other jobs."

"I agree," Mac said.

"The second part of the solution," Mac continued, "would be to allow the defense, in a trial, the right to introduce the *Constitution of the United States* into evidence. Juries should not only be informed that the *Constitution* is the law of the land, but shown that it says so right in the document. Then juries should be allowed to consider the *Constitution* when judging both their fellow citizens and the law itself.

"Third, there should be no more jury stacking. Juries should be drawn randomly from the population and they should represent the population. They should not be hand picked by either the prosecution or the defense. They are, after all, supposed to be representing all of us.

"This joke called *voir dire* is supposed to remove prejudiced jurors from the jury system. But everyone, and I mean virtually everyone in the system, knows it does exactly the opposite. Every defense attorney wants jurors who will let his client off while every prosecutor wants only jurors who will convict. And the state itself, through the judge, wants people who will, as they say, 'bring a verdict of guilty if the prosecution proves his case, even if the jurors disagree with the law.'"

"You know," Dave said, "I've heard judges say that telling jurors they can judge the law is jury tampering."

"Jury tampering is when you either coerce or bribe a juror to arrive at a specific verdict," Mac said. "Notifying a juror of his rights and duties isn't tampering. If it were, I truly believe that Adams, Jefferson, and the others I mentioned earlier would have known it and would have opposed jury nullification themselves.

"On the other hand," he continued, "telling jurors they must determine guilt or innocence only by the facts in the case, and not telling them they have both the right and the duty to judge the law, can be construed as tampering. It's lying to the jurors."

"And that puts the judge on the side of the prosecution," Dave said.

"That's right.

"So, no more tampering with the juries by the judges. Nor giving false instructions," Dave said.

"Right. Fourth, the jurors should know what sentence is going to be imposed if a verdict of guilty is brought. Would you bring a verdict of guilty for jaywalking if the penalty was a $25 fine? How about if the penalty was 10 years in jail?

"Fifth, and this is a biggie, civics classes in schools should stress jury rights. In the name of being good citizens, everyone graduating from high school should know what his powers and responsibilities are as a voter and a juror.

"And finally, it would be nice if journalists would reveal the truth about juries. There should be segments on *60 Minutes*, *First Edition*, and the evening news until it becomes so commonplace, no one bothers to make a big deal of it. In fact, it would be nice if that fellow on *20/20*, John Stossel, would do a piece on jury nullification."

"So, this is your solution," Dave said.

"It's a start. When the average citizen understands his rights and responsibilities as a juror, laws that infringe upon our rights will be all but impossible to enforce. Anyone who is able to get the ear of a legislator to have a dumb law passed will find that their fellow citizens, through juries, are going to disregard them.

"But not only will special interests find themselves unable to dictate to the majority, there also will be no dictatorship of the majority as minorities will find themselves empowered.

"And the last thing that would make the court system fairer in this country is if every prospective juror would familiarize him or herself with the *Constitution*, and especially the first 10 *Amendments*—the *Bill of Rights*—before assuming jury duty. That way unconstitutional laws would be impossible to enforce."

We arrived at the restaurant, and as we got out of the car, Mac said, "If only one juror out of 12 says, 'This or that law infringes on our rights, so I'm not going to convict anybody of violating it,' then laws like that will go away."

"Can we make this an election issue?" Dave asked.

"I don't know. Neither the Democrats nor the Republicans want jury nullification. Both parties represent special interests that do not want the average citizen throwing cases out of court. But it would be worth a try."

"Where do you think the government will intrude into our lives next?" Dave asked.

125

"I already know. The Internet."

"The Internet?" I asked as we walked into the restaurant.

"Yes, the Internet may be the greatest freedom tool since the invention of the printing press, and you can bet there are going to be attempts to control it."

With that we sat down.

"Let's not start talking about the Internet until we order," Dave said.

And with that we ordered lunch. Δ

Part VII

How the government wants to take control of the Internet and why a professional military is a danger to us all

Dave, Mac, and I arrived at a little restaurant in Brookings, Oregon, a city of some 5,000 people that lies about 30 miles south of Gold Beach on the southern Oregon coast where *Backwoods Home Magazine* is located.

Dave, of course, is Dave Duffy, the publisher of *Backwoods Home Magazine*, and Mac is O.E. MacDougal, our poker playing friend from southern California.

Since morning we'd been talking about the loss of freedoms in this country. Mac sounded pretty pessimistic. What he had been saying about the state of America since early that morning seemed pretty bad.

The waitress seated us and gave us menus, and now we sat poring over them.

Knowing Dave had eaten here before, I asked, "What's good?"

"All I've ever had here are the fish and chips—but they're great," he replied.

"That's all you eat here?" I asked. "Sounds to me like you're in a rut."

Mac put his menu down and said, "Fish and chips sounds good to me."

Dave still looked at the menu as if something else might catch his eye. But finally he said, "Yeah, I'm in a rut. I'll have the fish and chips, too." He put his menu on the table.

More on juries

I stared at my menu a while longer. I wondered what else might catch my eye. Then I heard Dave say to Mac: "On the way down here, you talked about the danger of letting the state, both the prosecution and the courts themselves—both of which are arms of the state—stack juries using *voir dire*. What about civil cases? Does the same thing apply there?"

"Absolutely. In civil cases, where lots of money is often at stake, lawyers want to get anyone who can think and anyone who's reasonable out of the jury box. They want emotional people whom they can lead. They want people who have or believe in a 'victim mentality'. And they absolutely don't want jurors who believe in individual responsibility.

"The result is that the average American has practically no representation in jury boxes in either criminal or civil cases.

"By literally handpicking jurors in civil cases, lawyers have left the rest of us baffled as to how they manage to get settlements that run into the hundreds of million of dollars and, more recently, into the billions of dollars. But it is through carefully crafted efforts to get only the most susceptible people on juries that the tobacco companies wind up with those judgments. And, of course, the cost of those judgments are almost always passed on to the consumer."

"But we need civil suits for when corporations are culpable," I said.

"Oh, I agree with you," Mac said. "But what I'm saying is, what's wrong with having the juries in civil cases represent a cross-section of the public. Is someone of the mind it would make the verdicts less fair? Stacking juries does not work in the public's interest."

"I don't think it's intended to be in the public's interest," Dave said.

Mac didn't say anything, but I could tell he agreed.

The solution

Dave continued. "So, I would imagine that the solution is to cut *voir dire* out of the courtroom, in both criminal and civil cases, and let the average citizen sit in the jury box and make these decisions, and not allow them to fall into the hands of the narrow-minded and susceptible juries handpicked by lawyers."

"I couldn't have said it better," Mac said. "Juries are supposed to be there to oversee the ways in which the laws are applied. It's supposed to be for all of us, not just the defendants and their lawyers. That has been the intent of juries since the *Magna Carta*. But today lawyers have found a way around it."

The Internet

We ate in silence for a while until Dave asked, "What were we actually going to talk about when we first arrived here? Oh, yeah, it was going to be about the Internet and the danger of government intrusion into it."

"What I said," Mac began, "was that the Internet may be the greatest freedom tool since the invention of the printing press. And I also said it was safe to bet that there are going to be attempts by the government to control it."

"Why didn't they just start out with controls?" Dave asked.

"Because the Internet and the Worldwide Web grew so fast that government was caught by surprise. There's a lot of inertia in government. Imposing controls now is going to be difficult. People know what a Web that is free from government control is like, and they like it. It's not going to be easy for the government to impose themselves upon it. The way things are happening now is nothing like it was a hundred years ago with automobiles."

"What do you mean?" I asked. "What do automobiles have to do with it?"

"Well, a hundred years ago automobiles were just playthings of the rich. The multitudes didn't own them so they didn't care when bureaucrats and politicians thought to cash in on them by taxing them. In contrast, at that time many people owned horses and carriages for transportation. Had the government tried to register and regulate them the way they did cars and trucks, there would have been a revolt. So the taxes and other controls were instituted early. By the time their use became widespread, people getting their first cars had no memory of what it was like when motor vehicle ownership was unencumbered by licensing and registration.

"Contrast that with the Internet. It grew fast, many people got on it early, and everyone has become accustomed to the freedom it's given them. It's now going to be difficult for the government to control it.

"But those who are looking to make their bailiwick the control of the Internet are always looking for inroads, they're always looking for something that will provide an excuse to control it. One of the things they've tried to do is create hysteria. They scream about porn, Internet casinos, terrorists, the handicapped and disabled, class warfare, the need to collect e-taxes on e-businesses, etc., etc., in the hopes that eventually some of those things will catch on."

"Disabilities?" Dave asked. "How are people using disabilities to control the Internet?"

"People have testified before Congress that the federal government should monitor and control the Worldwide Web in the name of the disabled. They have claimed everything from the need that the blind have access to the Web by mandating all Web pages have sound for their text to insisting on color schemes so that the color blind are not discriminated against."

"You're kidding," Dave asked.

"No I'm not. And what this could lead to is licensing of Internet sites, along with greater costs to put a site on line, and the disappearance of individual Internet sites unless they are government compliant."

"Regulation of the Internet," Dave said.

"Yes. But the problem, from the point of view of today's would-be regulators, is that the Web has grown so fast that there would be a lot of resistance to instituting much of this. But believe me when I say this: there are bureaucrats and politicians who are always trying to get control of it. And there are always citizens who are cheering them on."

I said, "I saw this thing that the Postal Service wants to charge five cents an e-mail to make up for lost revenue and..."

"That was a hoax that started in Canada," Mac said.

I stopped in surprise. "It was?"

"Yeah, it was," Dave said. "I checked it out when I first got an e-mail like that a couple of years ago."

"It's taken on the status of urban legend," Mac said.

I was still a little too surprised to speak.

"But it points to a good thing," Mac said, "because, when that e-mail was circulating, Congressmen were inundated with letters and e-mails protesting the postal charges. And when we get to your question, 'What's the solution,' that *is* the solution, namely, people have got to protest these intrusions.

"Furthermore, there are more important intrusions already happening and we should absolutely be protesting them before they become institutionalized. Though it may be too late, already."

"What are you talking about?" Dave asked.

"*Echelon* and *Carnivore*."

"What are those?" I asked.

"They are surveillance efforts on the part of government. Our government.

"*Echelon* is a project—actually a spy system—that has been around for quite some time. It's probably the most powerful intelligence gathering tool in the world. It was designed and is run by the National Security Agency, or NSA as it's called, and one of the problems with it is that the NSA was established by a presidential directive and is not subject to congressional review."

"This goes back to *Executive Orders* and how the President can act on pretty much anything simply by declaring an 'emergency.'" Dave said.

Mac nodded. "But unlike other intelligence gathering operations that are directed against foreign military targets, *Echelon* is directed against non-military targets that include not only other governments but businesses, organizations, and individuals in every country in the world including this one. It's an extreme threat to the privacy of people all over the world. Or, more to the point, it's an extreme threat to *our* privacy."

"How does this *Echelon* work?" Dave asked.

"It captures most, if not all, of the incredible volume of satellite, microwave, cellular, and fiber-optic traffic worldwide."

"What good can all that data be," I asked. "It seems like it would be impossible to sort through it all."

"Well, after gathering it, the next step they take is to use computers to filter, process, sort, and flag it."

"What are they looking for?" Dave asked.

"Who knows? Anything? Everything? But the real concern is that not only do very few people seem to be aware of its existence, but apparently there is no oversight by the courts, the Congress, or us—the people. We have no choices and we have no say. And at this point I don't think anyone outside of NSA even knows whether *Echelon* is being used illegally to spy on private citizens.

"The other threat is called *Carnivore*. It's an FBI project. It's a combination of hardware and software your Internet Service Provider—or ISP—must allow the FBI to install on their site. It's used to read all incoming and outgoing e-mails, and it notes who the sender and recipients are, what the message's subject is about, and what's in the body of the message. It also monitors the web-surfing and downloading habits of *all* of the ISP's customers. It even monitors instant messaging, newsgroups..." He paused. "You name it, it will monitor it."

"Where'd they get the name *Carnivore*?" I asked.

"It was a name the FBI now regrets because of its predatory connotation. But they came up with it because of what they considered its ability to get at the 'meat' of whatever they considered to be suspicious communications or Internet activity.

"The danger is that both of these efforts are in direct conflict with what the *Constitution* allows the federal government to do, and they are a direct violation of our rights as reflected in the *Bill of Rights*, including our right to be protected against warrantless searches.

The solutions

"So, along with e-mailing your Congressman, when you ask me about a solution to this problem, add that you should talk with your ISP and find out whether or not they have allowed the FBI to install *Carnivore* on their system, and yell like hell if they have or if they're considering it."

"I've heard some people talk about using encryption devices when sending e-mail. How do you feel about that?" Dave asked.

"The government has been opposed to individuals having access to good encryption programs and have said that if you're going to use one, they want to make it a law that you must give them the 'key' to it. The key means a way for them to read your messages even though they're encrypted. They don't mind you having privacy, they just don't want you to have it from them."

"Do you use an encryption program when you're on the Net?" I asked.

Mac smiled. "No, but I have looked into it. And anyone interested in finding out about them can use one of the search engines on the Web and look for PGP, which stands for Pretty Good Privacy, and find out all about them."

"Is there something better than 'pretty good privacy?'" I asked. "It sounds to me as though you'd want something called *really* good privacy."

"The use of the phrase 'pretty good' is an understatement. It's actually the the most secure and most convenient privacy you can get for use on the Web."

"How big do you think the dangers are of the government controlling the Internet or the Web?" Dave asked.

"Actually, users of the Internet and the Web have been spectacularly successful in resisting government control of it...so far. The Internet and the Web may be the last great bastion of freedom. Even the Chinese, those great squelchers of freedom, have found the Web difficult and cumbersome to control and, in the end, they may discover that even they are incapable of managing it."

"But they won't stop trying, will they," Dave said.

"No, they won't," Mac said. "One of the sad things is that every time there's a crisis, politicians, bureaucrats, and self-appointed demigods jump up to claim we have too many freedoms or that some freedoms must be sacrificed to ensure security. Others challenge these views and point out that not only are our freedoms worth defending, freedom itself is often the solution to a problem.

"For instance, a well-armed populace would stop the rampages of psychopaths or the malevolent intentions of these international terrorists that concern us so much. But the media is all too often statist and it voices only the opinions those who want to squelch freedom. And all too often, the only hearing they give to those who advocate freedom is when they interview certified kooks. They all too willingly ignore voices of reason that champion freedom."

"Who do you think they should interview to counter government spokesmen who say we have to give up some of our freedoms to obtain security?" Dave asked.

"The Libertarian Party, *Jews for the Preservation of Firearms Ownership*, Vin Suprynowicz, Claire Wolfe...there are a bunch of others.

"It used to be that these voices were hard to find. But because of the Internet, nowadays they can be heard. The Internet may be the single biggest weapon for freedom we have today.

"There was a time when the press viewed itself as the defender of freedom, but today the Internet has replaced the press as the source of the voices of dissent."

Dave said, "And so you're saying that the solution is vigilance on the part of Internet users..."

"And use the 'send' button on your e-mailer to tell your Congressman to stay away from the Internet," I added.

"And seriously consider using one of the PGP encryption programs," Dave added.

"I can't imagine any other solutions," Mac said. "If we want a free Internet, *we* have got to keep it free ourselves."

Large standing armies

The waitress brought us our lunches.

"Have you got any Tabasco sauce?" Mac asked. "And extra tartar sauce?" he called as she walked away.

We picked at our fries and I noticed Mac was eating his with the tartar sauce.

Looking up at me he said, "I like them this way better than I do eating them with ketchup."

I tried a few with tartar sauce. I liked them better that way.

The waitress returned with the hot sauce and, one by one, we slathered it on our fish.

"What else do you see as a threat to our freedoms?" Dave asked Mac between bites.

"There are a lot of things, some more important than others, but one of the biggest problems that confronts Americans right now is the drastic change we've seen in our military in the last 60 years. It's a change that doesn't seem to concern too many of us, but it should."

"What are you talking about?" Dave asked.

Washington's warning
against foreign entanglements

Observe good faith and justice towards all nations; cultivate peace and harmony with all...The nation which indulges towards another a habitual hatred or a habitual fondness is in some degree a slave. It is a slave to its animosity or to its affection, either of which is sufficient to lead it astray from its duty and its interest. Antipathy in one nation against another disposes each more readily to offer insult and injury, to lay hold of slight causes of umbrage, and to be haughty and intractable, when accidental or trifling occasions of dispute occur. Hence, frequent collisions, obstinate, envenomed, and bloody contests. The nation, prompted by ill-will and resentment, sometimes impels to war the government, contrary to the best calculations of policy. The government sometimes participates in the national propensity, and adopts through passion what reason would reject; at other times it makes the animosity of the nation subservient to projects of hostility instigated by pride, ambition, and other sinister and pernicious motives. The peace often, sometimes perhaps the liberty, of nations, has been the victim...It is our true policy to steer clear of permanent alliances with any portion of the foreign world...

George Washington
Farewell Address
September 19, 1796

"The military is just too big."

"Too big?" Dave asked.

"Yes. Traditionally there was never a large standing peacetime army in this country until 1945..."

"There wasn't?" I interrupted.

"No."

"Why not?"

"Our Founding Fathers didn't want a large standing army, especially a large *professional* standing army. And until the 1940s most Americans didn't want any large army hanging around in times of peace. But things have changed since World War II. We've had a large standing army ever since then, and we've gotten used to it just like it's always been here."

"But how did the Founding Fathers think we were supposed to defend ourselves?" I asked.

"In times of war they knew there wouldn't be a problem raising an army from the citizenry and, as it's turned out, they were right."

"But what was their reasons for not wanting a large army all the time?" I persisted.

"They feared them."

"They did?" Dave asked. "Why?"

"They were educated men and they knew, historically, that large standing armies don't *stand* around very long. They get used. They're sent off on foreign adventures that drain the treasury.

"Second, they saw that large standing armies have often become the accomplices of tyrants. Since the dawn of recorded history we know governments have used them as tools of suppression against the populations of their own countries.

"They also had the benefit of seeing what was happening in Europe in their own time, the late 1700s. They saw there were large armies all over Europe and those armies were the enemies of freedom.

"And, finally, they saw how their own government, the government of England—and you've got to remember that, until the Revolutionary War, our Founding Fathers were Englishmen—turned the English army against them over tax matters."

"I still think we need an army," I said.

"I didn't say we don't," Mac replied. "But the plan of our Founding Fathers was that this country should keep a navy intact at all times—and today they would no doubt also include an air force—along with a small core of professional soldiers, and the militia. And here I'm using the word *militia* in the way it's used in the Second Amendment, meaning the body of citizenry who can be called to arms, not the National Guard or some other professional organization."

"But that was then. Times have changed," I said.

"Times haven't changed that much," Mac responded. "Our Founding Fathers aren't the only people to feel this way. Even in our own life-times, there have been warnings about a permanent massive military establishment in peacetime. Dwight Eisenhower, the man who led the Allied forces during World War II and then became President in 1953, worried about what was happening with the increased growth in the military and its marriage to corporate America *after* World War II."

"He did?" Dave asked.

"Yes. Three days before he left office, in 1961, he gave his *Farewell Address*. In it he warned Americans against the military-industrial complex. He didn't like what was happening there. And keep in mind he wasn't some over-the-hill hippy or peacenik. Ike had made the military his career. He was there between the two World Wars when there was only a small core of professionals in the army. Then he watched as, in World War II, this country raised an army from the citizenry that was the most formidable military machine ever to wage a war. So he knew what it was like both before we inflated our defense establishment and when it became monolithic, as it is today. And it worried him."

"So what did he say in his speech?" Dave asked.

"He warned us about the dangers of a large permanent military estab-lishment, in particular one wedded to corporate America. He said that it would become a constant threat to our freedoms. He told us we had to watch the military-industrial complex closely."

"Have we?" Dave asked.

"No, we haven't."

"But a citizen army wouldn't be enough today," I said. "We have too many commitments."

"It *would* be enough if we stopped meddling in the affairs of other countries and if we stopped playing world policeman," Mac said.

"George Washington, in his own *Farewell Address*, warned us against foreign entanglements. He advised us that we should maintain our civility with foreign nations, but we should avoid permanent alliances with all of them. There was a time when school children had to memorize that speech and until the waning days of World War II Americans took his advice to heart and avoided most of the entanglements that had sucked European countries into the series of intramural wars they are so fond of."

Dave asked, "After World War II our army still depended on a draft which, in many ways, means it was still a citizen army. Then it suddenly went professional. What do you think prompted that?" he asked Mac.

"Resistance to the war in Vietnam," Mac said. "By and large, the American people didn't want involvement in Vietnam. In particular, the young—those who were bring drafted to fight and die there—didn't want it. They didn't see the point in our being in Vietnam, they didn't see the Vietnamese as a threat to us, and they didn't see us trying to win the war. Though, as the war wore on, they also didn't see *why* we wanted to win it.

"And who knows how much longer it could have gone on? But, of course, it didn't. It became the first war in our history, and maybe the first war ever, that was stopped by the citizenry. Primarily, it was the young and college students—the very people who were going to have to go fight it—who put the brakes on it. But they were citizens, nonetheless. And I want you to keep that in mind when you ask for a solution to the existence of a large standing army, as I know you will."

Dave smiled.

"In the meantime, the guys in the field—those fighting in Vietnam—gave their all. And, in case no one was keeping score, they never lost a major battle. But by the time it was over, the United States became the first and only country in history to lose a war without *ever* losing a major battle.

"But if we'd had a professional army back then, it's highly unlikely there would have been any protests to that illegal war. And now, for as long as we have a professional army, there will never again be protests against insane wars."

"Why did you just call the war in Vietnam an illegal war?" I asked.

"Because what happened in Vietnam wasn't *officially* a war."

"What do you mean it wasn't? People fought and died in it."

"But it wasn't a declared war," Mac said. "It is officially categorized as a *conflict*, just as Korea was, because it was conducted under *Executive Orders* without war ever being formally declared by Congress.

"Desert Storm, Panama, Granada, and everything else we've been involved with since September 2, 1945 have not been wars."

"What do you mean by all of this?" I asked. I don't understand what you're talking about.

Mac said, "The *Constitution* reserves the right to declare war *only* to the Congress and by the terms of the *Constitution* the President cannot unilaterally decide to send the nation off into battle. However, as I said earlier, Congress signed away many of its powers as well as the rights and the powers that the citizenry have had to run this country *through* the Congress. It did this when it gave presidents, beginning with FDR, the right to conduct themselves in any way they wish as long as he, the sitting President, claimed a *state of emergency* existed."

"Then you're saying that legally *only* the Congress can declare war," I said.

"Yes. The President, in his capacity as the Chief Executive, as provided for in *Article II, Section 2* of the *Constitution*, is tasked with overseeing a war, but he can't declare it. He's not supposed to commit American lives to wars the way ancient kings, emperors, and dictators did—except, of course, that he can do it now because Congress signed away their control about 70 years ago.

"Otherwise, *Article I, Section 8*, which declares the rights and powers of the Congress, states it is only the Congress that can declare a war. It is through the Congress that the will of the people is supposed to be enacted. Ultimately, we are the ones who are supposed to decide which wars Americans are willing to go off to fight and die in. But that's not the way it happens anymore. And we haven't fought in a war our Founding Fathers would declare *legal* since September 2, 1945, the day we accepted Japan's formal surrender. Yet, we've fought, bombed, and invaded countries since then. The President simply declares an *emergency* and sends in the troops."

"And the people no longer have any say," Dave said.

"That's right. And tens of thousands of Americans have died. At the same time, Americans have killed more foreign soldiers and civilians since World War II than we have in any declared war we've fought in, other than World War II.

"Further, I predict that the United States will *never* fight a declared war again for the rest of its history."

"And if we get into another Vietnam, will there be protests?" Dave asked.

"Protests on the scale we saw in the '60s and '70s will never happen in this country again. Those who protested over Vietnam did so because *they* were the fodder sent off to fight in that military adventure. Congress didn't want a war bad enough to declare one and the people didn't want one either. But the President did and the military is tied to him because he's the Commander in Chief.

"But because today we have this professional army, I predict we will never see large scale protests over a war ever again."

"You're saying Congress couldn't stop the Vietnam War," I said.

"The Congress tried several times to limit, alter, or stop what was going on over there. But they never succeeded because they no longer had the *legal* authority. They had signed it away a generation before.

"I suppose," he continued, "to some people that this investing of greater powers in one man, the President, represents some kind of progress, but to me it's a giant step backward to the ages of kings, emperors, and dictators."

The solution

"Okay..." Dave started to say

"...what's the solution?" Mac said.

"You read my mind," Dave said.

"I told you earlier the first thing we have to do is get rid of or limit the use of emergency powers by the President. But the next part of the solution is to stop playing world policeman. Even in the darkest days of the Cold War, the British, French, and West Germans could have taken care of themselves.

"I'd also like to see us go back to a citizen army. An army like we used to have, and which served us so well for about two centuries, one that is based on service by the citizenry, places restraints on the Executive Branch of our government. It is much more difficult for a President to engage in foreign adventures when it's the everyday citizen he's sending. Presidents Johnson and Nixon both discovered this.

"I'd also like to see us adopt a Swiss-type of military system."

"What's that?" I asked.

"Switzerland is one of the smallest European countries in both area and population. But on paper it has the largest military in Europe, over 400,000 soldiers, out of a population of about 6,000,000 citizens. I use the phrase 'on paper' because not all of them are on duty at any given time. In fact, at any time you can expect to find only 5,000 to 10,000 on active duty in the Swiss military.

"The way it works is that all young men go through 15 weeks of basic military training and then, for the next few decades, they all attend training camps for two or three weeks each year. The result is that, for all practical purposes, all Swiss men are in the military. But the irony is that the Swiss neither fight wars nor do they meddle in the affairs of other countries. You can't get 30 and 40-year-olds to go off and fight senseless wars. But you *can* get them to defend their homeland.

"And no one, including Hitler, wanted to invade Switzerland, a country where the citizens were prepared to dynamite every point of entry

Eisenhower's warning
of the military-industrial complex

Until the latest of our world conflicts, the United States had no armaments industry. American makers of plowshares could, with time and as required, make swords as well. But now we can no longer risk emergency improvisation of national defense; we have been compelled to create a permanent armaments industry of vast proportions. Added to this, three and a half million men and women are directly engaged in the defense establishment. We annually spend on military security more than the net income of all United States corporations.

This conjunction of an immense military establishment and a large arms industry is new in the American experience. The total influence—economic, political, even spiritual—is felt in every city, every State house, every office of the Federal government. We recognize the imperative need for this development. Yet we must not fail to comprehend its grave implications. Our toil, resources and livelihood are all involved; so is the very structure of our society.

In the councils of government, we must guard against the acquisition of unwarranted influence, whether sought or unsought, by the military-industrial complex. The potential for the disastrous rise of misplaced power exists and will persist.

We must never let the weight of this combination endanger our liberties or democratic processes. We should take nothing for granted. Only an alert and knowledgeable citizenry can compel the proper meshing of the huge industrial and military machinery of defense with our peaceful methods and goals, so that security and liberty may prosper together.

Dwight D. Eisenhower
Farewell Address
January 17, 1961

into their country and where every able-bodied man has a military rifle in his home, cans of ammo with which to feed it, and the training to use it.

"The result is that, as long as the Swiss have such a system, they are incapable of getting involved in foreign adventures like we did in Vietnam, and no one messes with them.

"Can you imagine Lyndon Johnson having sold the country on getting involved in Vietnam or Nixon keeping us over there four years after promising to get us out in the 1968 presidential campaign, if it had been 30 and 40-year-olds going and not just a bunch of kids fresh out of high school and college?"

"But we got 30 and 40-year-olds to go to the Middle East for Desert Storm," I said.

"Yes, 30 and 40-year-olds in a professional army. A tyrant can always get a professional army to do your bidding. What I'm talking about is a citizen's army."

But I thought you were against large standing armies," I said.

"I am," Mac replied.

"Well, it sounds like, on a per capita basis, Switzerland has the largest army in the world."

"It doesn't," Mac said. "What they have is, in effect, the largest militia in the world. And that's what the Founding Fathers wanted, a militia. They wanted free *citizens* to stand ready to defend their country, not a professional army."

"There's a lot of calls to use the military for police actions, especially in the War on Drugs or to combat terrorism," Dave said. "What do you think of that?"

"Using the military for police actions within our borders would be a terrible mistake."

"Why?" I asked.

"Soldiers are not concerned with your rights. You're not going to get a *Miranda* warning and they're not going to wait for search warrants to break down doors and look for...well, whatever they look for."

"What about terrorism?" Dave asked.

"One of the problems with all these military forays we've taken—Vietnam, Iraq, Bosnia, etc.—is that we may eventually find revenge played out against us with war or in the form of escalated terrorism on our home front. And the irony is, if terrorist attacks are successful, there will be a clamor in Congress to relieve us of our basic rights. But I've said before that the best way to defend our freedoms is by *using* our freedoms, not by resorting to self-imposed tyranny."

"But how can we protect ourselves from armed terrorists?" I asked.

"Let me tell you a story," he began. "One of the problems Israelis had was that terrorists began attacking their schools. Both students and teachers were taken as hostages or just outright killed. There seemed to be no solution.

"What were the Israelis going to do, place cops or soldiers in every school? I suppose they could have. But they hit on a much simpler and more effective solution and it was a very *American-like* solution. They simply let teachers arm themselves if they wanted. It wasn't mandatory, it was optional, but quite a few teachers availed themselves of the opportunity and suddenly terrorists were confronted with a dilemma: how do you attack a so-called victim who's going to whip out a gun and kill you? And how do you tell the unarmed victims from those who are carrying heat?

"The result was that terrorism at the schools fell to zero, except for one foray into Jordan where a group of students, teachers, and chaperones took a field trip to a place near the Jordanian border ironically called the 'Zone of Peace.' The Jordanian government requested that the Israeli teachers and chaperones not bring their guns. So, out of respect, they didn't. But the terrorists learned about this and they also showed up and had a field day. It is, as far as I know, the only time Israeli teachers have willing disarmed themselves and it is also the only time I know of that terrorists have successfully targeted students and teachers since teachers started arming themselves."

"So, what's your final word on the military and national defense?" Dave asked.

Mac thought for a few moments. We were nearly done eating and the waitress had already dropped the check on the table. Mac grabbed it.

"I've got it," Dave said reaching for his wallet.

Mac shook his head and placed a credit card with the check which the waitress scooped up as she went by. "Let me get it this time," he said.

Then he was quiet. But, finally, he said, "My final word. Let me say this, I'm no admirer of Theodore Roosevelt, but there's one thing he said that I've taken to heart. He said, 'Speak softly and carry a big stick.' I'd make a foreign policy for this country by melding this with the essence of Washington's *Farewell Address* in which he warned against foreign entanglements. We'd be civil and courteous to all other nations, but if they mess with us, that's what the stick is for."

The waitress brought back the receipt and Mac added a tip, totaled the figures, and signed the bottom. Then we stood to leave.

"Is there anything else we should be concerned with?" Dave asked.

"There are plenty of things. But one of the things we should be concerned with is understanding the political change that's taken place in this country and how it's changing how we perceive freedom. And that we have become a fascist country without realizing it."

"How could we become fascist without realizing it?" Dave asked.

"Because people don't understand what fascism is. In the schools we have teachers defining fascism to their students as intolerance or equating it to the concentration camps the Nazis set up. It's not."

We walked out of the restaurant and got in Dave's car. Dave had some errands to run before we returned to the offices up in Gold Beach. Δ

Part VIII

America as a fascist country: how it became that way, how it interferes with our freedoms, and who's to blame

There were three of us—Dave Duffy, O.E. MacDougal, and me—in Dave's car as we returned from Brookings, Oregon, to the magazine's offices in Gold Beach. Dave, of course, is the publisher of *Backwoods Home Magazine* and Mac is our poker-playing friend from southern California.

Most of the day the three of us had been discussing the steady loss of freedoms in this country. Mac thinks the losses will continue and that they've been getting worse for the last several decades. He even thinks a dictatorship is possible in this country and could happen within the lifetimes of the three of us.

The ride was uneventful because Mac, who had arrived at the office at 2 a.m. that morning and had slept briefly on the floor under one of the printers, was asleep again on the back seat.

We got to the office late in the afternoon and parked down back. Mac was still asleep and as Dave got out he said, "Let's let him sleep."

We did, and we went upstairs and back to work.

About an hour later I looked up and there was Mac coming in the front door. He carried a couple of bags.

"We decided to let you sleep," Dave said.

"I woke up when you guys closed the doors," Mac said. "I decided to go for a walk and I stopped down at one of the local stores." He put the bags on the table next to the refrigerator, then reached in one and pulled out a bottle. "Grapes, fermented," he said as he held it up. It was a bottle of merlot. He placed it on the table and reached back into the bag. "Deep-fried mushrooms," he said as he pulled out another package. He reached back in and pulled out something else.

"Grapes, seedless and unfermented," he said, and he was holding a bag of red seedless grapes.

"What's in the other bag?" Dave asked.

"I called Ilene," Mac said, referring to Dave's wife "and told her I'd make a chicken dish up at your house tonight. It's stuff for the recipe."

He popped the cork of the bottle. When he turned around Dave and I were standing behind him with wine glasses.

Pretty soon Dave and I were back at our desks while Mac was sitting in the stuffed chair.

Mac looked at me and said, "This has got to be the only job you've ever had where you're allowed to drink at your desk."

"Allowed?" Dave said. "It's expected."

The three of us laughed and raised our glasses in an impromptu toast. I sipped my wine. It was very good.

"Where'd we leave off?" Dave suddenly asked.

For a moment Mac didn't realize Dave was talking to him. When he did he looked confused for just a second.

"I think you were going to talk about how you think we've become a fascist country," I said.

Turning to Dave I said, "Isn't that the last of the things on his list that he said he thinks are leading to a dictatorship?"

"Yeah," Dave said.

"Oh, yeah," Mac said, and looked up at the ceiling as he thought for a moment. Then he began to nod. He took another sip of his wine.

"Do you really feel that we're going to become fascist?" I asked.

"We already have," he replied.

"How can you say that?" I asked. "If we were fascist, you wouldn't be able to say things like that."

"Things like what?" he asked.

"All the critical things you've said today."

"Why not?"

"Fascism means intolerance and concentration camps," I said.

What is fascism?

Mac thought again for a moment. Then he said, "What we should do is define our terms so we aren't talking about different things when we think we're talking about the same thing."

"What do you mean 'define terms'?" I asked.

"Define the 'isms.' Let's start out with communism. How would you define communism?" he asked.

I thought a second. "Well, in its theoretical sense, that's where private property has been eliminated—the state owns everything—and the state determines both the production and distribution of everything," I said.

"Good," he said. "Now, how would you define socialism?"

I was still thinking when Dave said, "I believe there are several kinds of socialism and, in reality, even communism can be defined as one of the types of socialism."

"That's right," Mac said. "Communism is actually the most extreme kind of socialism and it's where, as John said, the state owns and manages everything. Although it's never been perfectly implemented, where all private property was eliminated, it was implemented to a remarkable degree in the former USSR, modern China, Albania, North Korea, and several other countries. It turned out to be extremely inefficient, but one of its hallmarks is that all of the countries that adopted it have been dictatorships. Of course, Marx, the father of communism, advocated a dictatorship which he declared would eventually go away leaving a benign type of anarchy. But that's another story."

"Then what are the other types of socialism?" I asked.

"Well," Mac began, "one is state socialism, such as now exists in Sweden and was for a time a large part of the economic landscape in Great Britain. In state socialism the prime industries are owned by the state, but otherwise there is private property including private businesses. But under state socialism if a business becomes too successful...or maybe I should say, is perceived as *too important*...it becomes a candidate to be taken over by the state.

"Last, there's fascism, sometimes called national socialism, in which most or all of the businesses and services remain in private hands but they are guided or directed by politicians and bureaucrats in the employ of the state.

"There are other variants of socialism, such as utopian socialism and guild socialism, among others, but basically, from an economic standpoint, there are just three main types: communism, where the state owns everything; state socialism, where the state owns the major or important industries; and national socialism, or fascism, where the state owns no industry, but in varying degrees controls what's otherwise private."

"Communism, socialism, and fascism," Dave said.

"That's right," Mac said. "I think you'd get most economists to agree these are workable definitions and it's pretty much historically accurate as far as socialist movements go."

"Then there's capitalism," Dave said.

"Yes. But whereas in the variants of socialism there are bureaucrats and politicians deciding the direction the economy should go in, in pure capitalism it's market forces that determine what happens. And, of course, unlike the various kinds of socialism, which are both economic and political theories, capitalism is just an economic theory."

"There's no 'capitalist party' ticket. No doctrine of capitalistic social thought," Dave said.

"No," Mac said. "And, as for fascism being about concentration camps and intolerance," he said looking at me, "you're thinking about the Nazis. Fascism was adopted by many countries and Mussolini and the Italians were the first to institute it.

"The Germans—specifically, the Nazis—adopted it later and they were the ones who added the concentration camps. But the Nazis didn't need fascism to build concentration camps and concentration camps are not one of the defining characteristics of fascism any more than they are a defining characteristic of communism or capitalism.

"As far as I know, during World War II not only Germany, but two of the other combatants had concentration camps for their own citizens. Others may have had prisoner of war or P.O.W. camps, but only three had concentration camps."

"Which are the other two?" Dave asked.

"The former Soviet Union and the United States."

"What!" I said.

"The Soviet Union had them for political enemies of the state and malcontents. They were called labor camps or gulags. And the United States had two kind of concentration camps—internment camps for Japanese-Americans during the war, and Indian Reservations, which are the longest running concentration camps in the world."

"We spoke about that earlier," Dave said.

Mac nodded. "We did," he said.

I didn't say anything, but I still felt uncomfortable calling Indian Reservations concentration camps, though Mac assured me a great many Indians would agree with him.

He continued. "Today, we've equated fascism with Hitler and so-called right wing governments such as the military dictatorships in Argentina and Chile, as well as with the Nazi concentration camps of World War II. But I'd be surprised if one person in a hundred realized that fascism is simply an economic and political theory."

"But fascism is evil," I protested.

"To whom?" Mac asked. "To the average German living in Germany from 1933 to the end of World War II, neither National Socialism nor

Hitler were evil. He was both a savior and a hero to millions. To the average Jew, to the average gypsy, to homosexuals, and political dissidents, and to much of the rest of the world, he was an evil tyrant. But not to most Germans.

"The same goes for Mussolini in Italy. He was, for a time, not only a hero in his own country, but admired by much of the world."

"But how can you call fascists socialists?" I asked. "Socialism is a left wing philosophy. Everyone knows fascism is a right wing philosophy."

"Right wing and left wing don't mean an awful lot," Mac said. "Initially, fascism was seen as a left wing ideology by those who saw themselves on the left. And since it was largely left-leaning people who were in power during World War II, they chose not to refer to the fascists as socialists any longer, so they lumped the fascists with the rest of their political enemies who were on the right."

"You're saying the terms are artificial?" I asked.

"Yes. It's like 'newspeak' in George Orwell's novel, *1984*, in which terms shift meanings overnight to suit political ends. It happened again recently. Western liberals now refer to Russia's old-line communists as 'right-wingers.' About 10 years ago they decided to distance themselves from them because the 'dictatorship of the proletariat' had become passé and democracy was now *in*. Immediately forgotten was that for decades Soviet communists—and by extension, Russian communists—along with their dictatorship, were the darlings of liberals in the West *because* they were the ultimate 'leftists.' Now that they were no longer popular, they were relegated to the right virtually overnight. And just as was done in the novel *1984*, not one American news commentator noted the change. It was just as if it had always been that way."

"I remember when we talked about that before," Dave said. (See "What's left, what's right? What's liberal, what's conservative?" available in *A Backwoods Home Anthology, The Ninth Year*.)

"But the truth is that, just as with Hitler and the Nazis, the old-line communists hadn't changed a bit. It was the Western liberals who had changed. So who knows what they're going to be calling left wing tomorrow.

"If you've never read the novel *1984*, you should. If you haven't read it in quite awhile, it's worth rereading now. You think that what happens in Oceania, the country of the protagonist, Winston Smith, could never happen here. But it does with alarming frequency.

"But if you think about it, the difference between left wing and right wing is artificial. Those on both the right and the left ask for more government control and more government intrusion; they just ask for it in different areas. It's the reason Libertarians have so much trouble recruiting from the ranks of Democrats and Republicans, because they both advocate some kinds of government presence in everyday life whereas Libertarians want the government out of their lives.

"The real difference in American politics is not between left and right or Democrat and Republicans in America. The real difference is between those who want government controls and those who do not. And there aren't too many in the latter camp, so you don't hear much of anything about them."

Dave got up, grabbed the bottle, and poured us all a little more wine.

"What was the attraction of fascism as opposed to other flavors of socialism?" Dave asked.

"Fascism's roots go back a long way. But it didn't become a systematic theory until around the time of World War I and it really didn't make much of an impact until the Depression of the 1930s. Then, many of its ideas, especially its economic ideas of leaving production in private hands while directing it by the state, swept the world."

"Why did it take hold then?" Dave persisted.

"Because of the Depression, people were looking for scapegoats and saviors, villains and heroes. They were looking for leaders who had— or claimed to have—solutions. Intellectuals, politicians, and bureaucrats loved the concept provided by fascist economic ideas: central planning without having to confiscate private property.

"So out of the debris of the Depression arose men like Roosevelt and Hitler. Each created the impression that he was ending the Depression within his country."

"How can you compare Roosevelt to Hitler?" I asked. "Roosevelt ended the Depression."

"If you look at the history of both men, neither one of them ever saw two seconds of a good economy during their tenures in office."

"But Roosevelt ended the Depression," I repeated.

"What are the hallmarks of a depression?" Mac asked.

"When massive amounts of people are thrown out of work," I said.

"That's one definition," Mac said. "So, let's work with it." He stood up and took the *World Almanac and Book of Facts* for the year 2000 from one of the bookshelves in the office. First he perused the index, then he leafed through the pages.

"Here are the unemployment figures for various years: 1929—3.2%"

"That's not depression figures," I said.

"1930—8.7%."

"That's getting up there," Dave said.

"1931—15.9%"

"Now we have depression," I said. "But wasn't Hoover still in office in 1931?"

Mac nodded. "Indeed he was. But now let's hear the rest of the figures: 1932—23.6%. 1933—24.9%"

"Wow, those figures are really up there," Dave said.

"It's in March of 1933 that FDR takes office," Mac said. "So his first year sees record unemployment."

"Yeah, but he hadn't had a chance to end it yet," I said. "It was just his *first* year."

Mac nodded again then continued to read: "1934—21.7%. That's the end of his second year.

"His third year is 1935 and unemployment is at 20.1%.

"1936—16.9% This is an election year and FDR is voted back into office.

"1937—14.3%."

"So, after five years the Depression goes on," Dave said.

"But it's getting better," I said. "Unemployment was falling."

Mac paused. "Yes, after five years in office unemployment had fallen to 1931 levels."

He continued. "1938—19.0%"

"Wait a minute," Dave said. "You mean unemployment went back up?"

"Yes. For all of his programs and policies, after six years in office, the Depression deepens again.

"1939—17.2%. 1940—14.6%. After eight years in office—as long as any President before him or since had served—he finally has unemployment back to what it was in Hoover's second year in office."

"Then why do they call it Hoover's Depression?" Dave asked. "It's beginning to sound like Roosevelt's Depression."

Mac shrugged.

I said nothing.

"There are no figures here for 1941," he said and closed the *Almanac*, "but that's the year we enter into World War II and we go into a wartime economy.

"So, at the beginning of his presidency there was unemployment and nothing to buy; then there was a wartime economy with people dying, but full employment—yet, there was still nothing to buy except for War Bonds which were conceived to help take money out of circulation."

"So what's your point?" Dave asked.

"My point is that fascist economic ideas were sweeping the world and Franklin Roosevelt used them, Mussolini used them, Hitler used them. In fact, almost everybody but the communists used them. With fascist economics politicians didn't have to nationalize industry, and private property could be left in private hands. But, at the same time, in this country Roosevelt laid the foundation for new and powerful federal bureaucracies that would begin to direct the economy and control the country.

"I also wanted to show that Roosevelt and his brand of socialism did not end the Depression, though he had adopted many of the fascist-like tools that were being developed at that time."

"Tools such as...?" Dave asked and let his question hang there.

"Keynesian economics, which is essentially a fascist-type of economic theory, invented by the Englishman John Maynard Keynes. It was adopted by politicians and bureaucrats because it gave them something *to do*. It empowered them while, once again, leaving property in private hands."

"How does Keynesian economic theory work?" Dave asked.

"The theory says the government must guide the economy through manipulation of the money supply and through fiscal programs. By adopting Keynesian ideas, governments in developed countries, such as the United States, were able to build huge bureaucracies to oversee it."

"But I still wonder why fascism was adopted and not communism, like the Soviet Union adopted?" Dave asked.

"It was the problem of private property. Confiscation of private property by the state was easier in Russia where the overwhelming majority of the population owned neither businesses nor real estate. But in countries like Italy, Germany, and the United States, communism wouldn't have gone over as well because of the numbers of people who owned private property. And in this country private property—at least back then—was an even bigger issue than in most European countries. This made fascism, which left property in private hands, palatable."

I had been sitting at my computer doing a quick search on the Web for other things about fascism.

"Hey," I interrupted, "one of the characteristics of fascism is nationalism. We don't have that," I said triumphantly.

156

"Actually we do. Sometimes it's subtle, sometimes it's blatant. Do you remember the quote by the Clintons: 'I don't understand how someone can say they love their country but hate their government.'? Or another by JFK: 'Ask not what your country can do for you, but what you can do for your country.'?

"The first quote identifies the government with the country. That's a hallmark of fascism. Our Founding Fathers understood what it was like to love their country while hating their government because, keep in mind, until July 4, 1776 they were Englishmen. To them their country and their government were separate issues. Today, hating your government while loving your country sounds like a contradiction because we've come to think of the two as one.

"The second quote, by JFK, ignores the possibility that this could be a nation of self-reliant individuals. It makes the assumption that the only choices available are between two types of socialism: that of the Swedes, and that of Mussolini and Hitler. The Swedes want to know what their country can do for them; the Nazis wanted to know what they could do for their country.

"Most of the Founding Fathers, the same people who wrote the *Constitution* and the *Bill of Rights*, would have thought both quotes were very European and not American at all."

"So you're saying we really are nationalistic."

"Yes, and although we have, at times, substituted the U.N. or the environment for the concept of 'the state,' make no mistake, they are only substitutions for some temporal power that is more important than the individual and to which the individual is always subject."

"Do you think we're just getting used to it?" Dave asked.

"Of course we are. That's why the *Bill of Rights* makes so many of us uncomfortable now."

"What do you mean?" I asked.

"The *Bill of Rights* is mostly about individuals and their rights. It puts the individual ahead of the state. People today have been conditioned to feel it's supposed to be the other way around."

Who wants fascism?

"If, as you say, we're becoming fascist, who is it that wants it that way?" Dave asked.

"It seems like everybody does."

"Not liberals," I said. "They're the ones most opposed to fascism."

"That's not true," Mac said. They're only opposed to the *term* fascism. They're not opposed to its ideas. For years you've no doubt heard people—liberals in particular—say that what we need is a blend of socialism and capitalism. Well, that's exactly what fascist economic theory is: the means of production—capitalism—left in private hands, but directed by the government. However, we don't use the word 'fascism' because it fell out of favor due to Hitler and Mussolini during World War II.

"Today, instead of fascists, many who espouse fascist economic policies call themselves progressives, liberal, greenies, environmentalists, corporate CEOs, the religious right, etc. None of them would dare call themselves fascists, even if they knew what fascism is. And, as I said before, I'll bet not one person in 100 knows what it is."

"Well, you're kind of making sense here," Dave said. "Everything from National Health Care to corporate subsidies is a blend of capitalism and socialism. But I guess I never thought too much about corporations wanting fascism. With each, companies remain private but under public control."

Mac nodded again.

"How do business leaders see this?" Dave asked.

"The cry for government intervention in business, by businessmen, goes at least as far back as the so-called robber barons."

"What do you mean?" Dave asked. "Why do you say 'so-called'?"

"The way we're taught in schools today, in the 19th century various men such as John D. Rockefeller, J.D. Hill, and Cornelius Vanderbilt were getting rich by stifling business and fleecing the public. In truth, those men, and others like them, built their businesses up by running them efficiently, cutting prices, and driving their competition—which in many cases were government subsidized businesses—out of business.

"There's an excellent book on this by Burton W. Folsom titled *The Myth of the Robber Barons*. It clearly shows that the campaign against the so-called robber barons wasn't conducted by consumers, but by their competitors. It was other businessmen, who couldn't run their businesses efficiently, who cried to Congress to intervene.

"This was all supposedly done to help the consumer. But when companies like Standard Oil, which were supposedly preying on the public, were broken up, prices didn't fall, they went up."

"So the roots of fascist-type economics in America go back much earlier than Mussolini and Hitler," Dave said.

"Yes," Mac answered.

"But there are still differences between what Mussolini and Hitler did and what American businesses wanted 100 years ago or what we want today," I said. "So it's not the same."

Mac shrugged. "Well, there's a difference between communist theory, the way Karl Marx and Friedrich Engels spelled it out, and what was practiced in the Soviet Union, China, North Korea, Albania, and numerous other places. The way each country adopted communism was unique to that country. But we never hesitated to call them all communist because the essential features of communism were there.

"And in the same way, Mussolini and Hitler practiced fascism differently, but I don't think anyone would say one or the other of them wasn't fascist.

"And in this country the features of fascism exist both economically and socially, but it's not exactly as practiced by the Germans or the Italians."

"So, in answer to the question, 'Who in America wants fascism...?'" Dave started to ask, and he left his question unfinished again. But we both knew what he was asking.

"Almost everyone," Mac answered.

"And you say that, even today, businesses want it, too?"

"Among the the most strident advocates of fascism are America's corporations."

"But businesses want capitalism," I said.

"Capitalism involves open markets and *laissez-faire* economic policies. In theory, it's the ultimate democracy and insists on private property and personal rights. But the way most businesses are run today often has little to do with capitalism because those companies want governmental favors and governmental protections. The trade-off is that with those favors and protections come government intervention and government force.

"In truth, when businesses make the plea for open markets and laissez-faire economic policies, when they say they don't want government interference, what they really mean is that they want the government off *their* backs because *they* want to do something that's going to make *them* money. On the other hand, they often want and ask for regulations and intervention when they want to *limit competition*. They want the government to ensure that other businesses are less competitive, or have to pay tariffs which make their products more expensive, or if an entrepreneur wants to start up a new company that will compete with them, they want the bar set so high that there are too many regulatory hurdles to overcome or so startup costs are so high that the entrepreneur can't compete.

"Other times, they ask for a government subsidy because they can't operate efficiently."

"So corporations will invite government to intrude as long as it turns them a buck," Dave said.

"That's right. They'll even embrace government principles and ideas when they're wrong, if it will enhance their bottom line."

"Can you defend a statement like that?" I asked. "Can you give us an example of a corporation embracing a government principle that's wrong just to get rich?"

"Sure. In their book *Silencing Science*, authors Steven Milloy and Michael Gouch give a good example involving DuPont and CFCs.

"When chlorofluorocarbons—the gases more commonly called CFCs that used to be used as an aerosol propellant and in air conditioners—were cited as depleters of the ozone layer, the first reaction of DuPont Corporation was to investigate whether there's any evidence that the ozone layer is in danger from CFCs. They did this because, along with several other companies, they made CFCs themselves and had a stake in selling them.

"What they discovered was that, though there were a lot of theories, there was no evidence to support the environmentalists' or government's claims. Or at least there was no evidence that would stand up to peer review among other scientists. But they knew that selling this argument was going to be difficult, especially since the media had already made up its mind that CFCs are a danger."

"So what did they do?" I said.

"They discovered something even more interesting. They held patents on gases that could be substituted for the CFCs. These new gases not only cost several times as much as CFCs, they also promised huge profits for the company because Dupont would be the sole source of the gases. So they not only gave in and were willing to stop the production of the CFCs, a product on which they did not have exclusive rights, they also became one of the loudest voices calling for the banning of CFCs. They knew that with government intervention, it would be impossible for competitors to sell much of the less expensive CFCs, thus ensuring Dupont both a monopoly and big profits."

"Rather than insisting that there be a scientific inquiry to determine the truth here, they went against their own scientific findings all for the bottom line?" Dave asked.

"DuPont, like any corporation, may use science to make its products, but it's not in the science business, and it's not in the business of selling truth. It's in business to make a profit, as well it should be.

"But don't blame just businessmen for this. Anytime someone, whether it's an individual, a group, or a corporation, demands some kind of law or regulation be enacted to control someone else, there are bureaucrats willing to step in and act on their behalf because this is how bureaucrats are empowered. This doesn't mean that everyone who wants an advantage provided to them gets their way, but it still happens with alarming frequency."

"Do you have other examples?" Dave asked.

"Farm subsidies which are supposed to benefit family farms are now laws benefitting agribusiness."

"But they also save family farms," I said.

"Yes, they do. But why? And are we supposed to save family businesses at public expense? Are we supposed to save every family-owned laundromat and gas station at public expense, too? If you can't run your laundromat or gas station competitively, then maybe you're in the wrong business. And that goes for farmers, too. Or are families that own farms somehow more sacrosanct than families that own gas stations?"

"But they grow our food," I said.

"In a country where we pay farmers *not* to grow things, there's a myth that unless we keep the most inefficient farmers in business we're going to starve," Mac said.

He continued. "Another example is our entire banking system, as it has been since 1933. It's a system of privately owned businesses run tightly under the direction of the federal government."

162

"Which is, according to the definition you've given us, fascist economics," Dave said.

Rights and crimes

"Well, you've made a case for the way fascism in this country may be infringing on our economic freedoms," Dave said. "What about our personal freedoms?"

Mac said, "First, keep in mind that your economic freedoms are part of your personal freedoms. Don't separate them out. Your economic freedoms have to do with your property rights. And all socialistic economic theories infringe on your property rights to some extent.

"But beyond this, in government-directed societies, not only are businesses managed, there's the management of people with phony rights and phony crimes."

"What do you mean by that?" I asked.

"We spoke earlier about the creation of new 'legal' rights that are not protections against the government, but entitlements that must be supplied by fellow citizens. (See Part II, *How the creation of new "legal" rights is destroying our real rights.*) Of course, this must be managed by the government.

"In the same way we have other laws meant to manage people. Everything from zoning laws to helmet and seat belt laws are meant to allow the government to manage individuals."

"Are you saying this is another manifestation of fascism?" Dave asked.

"I'm saying this is a manifestation of all societies that are 'government managed' which includes all of the socialisms."

"Hold on," I said. "In cases like seat belt laws, the state has a good argument. All too often it's the state that has to take care of you, and you can't just opt out of system. So the state has a right to dictate your behavior in certain cases, like wearing seat belts, where you may otherwise become a financial burden to it."

"Then you must also believe the state has a right to gun confiscation."

"How's that?"

"Gunshot victims, whether by accident or by crime, may become wards of the state. If government can outlaw anything that might cost it money, the *Second Amendment* becomes moot.

"Overweight?" he asked, staring pointedly at my gut. "That's a cause of heart disease and a potential drain on the public treasury. If the government wants us in better shape so it can save money, it makes obesity a crime. The state can then regulate what you eat and create forced exercise programs it will be a crime to avoid."

"Oh, don't be foolish," I said.

"Yesterday's foolishness becomes today's nightmares and crimes. There was a time when people would have laughed if you'd said ethnic slurs could become 'hate crimes' that resulted in stiffer prison sentences than physical assault, or that smoking on a plane could become a federal offense with jail time..."

"Or be fined for not wearing a seat belt," Dave said.

"What you've done, with your argument for seat belts," Mac continued, "is to put a price on our rights. If the government can find economic reasons, they're allowed to intrude in our lives. They create a system, make it illegal to opt out of it, then use that system against us. There's going to be more of it in the future."

"Make a prediction about that," Dave said.

Mac thought a second. "Today we laugh at the concept of the government forcing us to have a National ID Card that would be the equivalent of what the Nazis had when they insisted everyone 'have their papers.' But one day it will be a crime in this country not to have an ID Card on your person at all times."

"Are you saying that one day there won't be National ID Cards and the next they'll be throwing you in jail for not having one?" I asked.

"There'd be a revolt if they did it that way. So they won't institute them with prison sentences. They'll be instituted by bureaucrats. One day they'll institute them, and the next day you simply won't be able to get some services without the card. And day after day the card will become a requirement for more and more of the services you want, including opening a bank account, cashing a check, getting a driver's license, or getting a job. It's only after the overwhelming majority of us get used to them that there will be penalties for not having one. And by that time no one will come to help you because it'll seem harmless. You'll be a crank for not submitting and a criminal for not having one.

"In fact," he continued, "There will come a time when you cannot get on the Internet, including the Web, without a national ID code on your computer. It'll be the ultimate cookie."

"Says who?" I asked.

"Says me. It's my second prediction."

"You mean you've heard about this coming?" he asked.

"No. But I'll make a bet, it's coming soon.

"You heard it here, first," he added.

I didn't say anything. I was flabbergasted. I couldn't believe he'd be saying things like this, but Dave was unfazed.

"The government has been looking for ways to control the Internet, and this is how they'll do it. And not only will you not be able to get on without an ID, it'll be a crime to misrepresent your identity. And I know plenty of people who will think that this is a great idea."

"How will it come about?" Dave asked.

"They'll institute it with a crisis. It'll be a war, a terrorist attack, a means to catch pedophiles, to track deadbeat dads, or something for the War on Drugs. Maybe they'll use a combination of things. But it will be some kind of crisis because that's the only way they'll be able to get around the resistance that computer users have shown to government intrusion so far."

"The users will be gulled into believing it's for their benefit," Dave said.

Mac nodded. "That's how these things are often done."

I wasn't going to let this seat belt thing slip by. "But it's stupid not to wear a seat belt," I said.

Mac looked at me. "Oh, I agree," he said. "But when did not taking care of yourself become a crime in the United States?"

"Well, I just think there are times the government has to step in."

"And that's what socialism, and in particular, fascism are all about. Every form of socialism demands some kind of people management to keep the bureaucracies that sustain it both busy and supported. It doesn't matter whether it's communism, state socialism, or national socialism, they all do it. And when they start managing you, your rights, freedoms, and liberties become secondary. In fact, they become privileges."

He waited for a response from me. But I didn't say anything for a moment.

Finally, he said. "Under fascism, the state is a hero. To those who go along with the new agenda the government is again a hero. For example, zoning laws which usurp property rights, bureaucracies such as the FDA, which now claim dominion over your body, environmental controls which have also made property rights secondary, and plans for a national ID system to keep track of us. They convince us they are either saving us from ourselves or they are saving us from our neighbors.

"Almost every time they 'solve our problems for us' we pay for it with more of our rights. And they will use any argument they can. In the case of seat belts and motorcycle helmets, they use an economic argument. But in environmental arguments they are saving the world.

"We are managed, yet private property seems to stay in place and individual rights *seem* to stay intact. It's classic fascism. We don't call it fascism, and that's supposed to make it okay."

"You're saying this is like George Orwell's *1984*," Dave said. "In *1984*, the government isn't concerned with reality, it just has to change the appearance of reality by manipulating the common vocabulary."

"That's right," Mac said. "That's exactly what we've done: we've adopted fascism, but changed our vocabulary to hide it from ourselves."

166

"But a lot of the things the government does, it does to protect our freedoms," I said.

"Like what?" Dave asked me.

"Like instituting a National ID Card," I said.

"What do you say?" Dave asked Mac. "What about times when the government is doing things to protect our freedoms?"

"It can't," he replied.

"What do you mean?" Dave asked.

"There's been a subtle shift in belief in this country from a time when it was thought that protecting freedom was an individual responsibility to now, when it's assumed that protecting freedom is a government function."

"It should be both." I said.

"It can't be," Mac replied. "Most of the freedoms we have are *freedoms from government*. George Washington said, 'Government is not reason, it is not eloquence—it is force.' Freedom of speech, freedom of worship, the right to keep and bear arms, the right to a jury trial, and a host of other things...every one of those is freedom from government intrusion. We can't expect to depend on the potential oppressor to save us from himself. We, the citizens, must do that for ourselves.

"When the government says it's going to protect us, even when it says it's protecting our freedoms, it always expects us to give up some of our freedoms as a price. And the freedoms we're asked to give up are always the very freedoms meant to protect us *from* them."

It was 5 p.m. and everyone else at the magazine was preparing to go home.

"We should get out of here," Dave said and he started shutting down his computer.

I started shutting mine down, too.

Mac went to the refrigerator to get the wine.

"I'll put that bag in my trunk," I said. "It's going to be regarded as an open container if we get stopped."

"I was wondering what to do with it," Mac said. "I guess this means you'll be going up to Dave's house and joining us for supper."

"I wouldn't miss it for the world," I said. I know how Mac cooks.

Is there a solution?

"What can we do about it?" Dave suddenly asked.

"About fascism?" Mac asked.

Dave nodded. "That and the possibility of a dictatorship in this country."

"The trouble is, almost all of us now have a stake in keeping things the way they are. And though we've put a lot of things in place to make a dictatorship possible, no one really wants to change the status quo. We're afraid to."

"But there's got to be something," Dave said.

"You've been asking for solutions to each of these things I've said are possible threats to our freedoms, from the government stacking of juries to presidential rule by *Executive Orders*. And I keep suggesting possible solutions. But neither of you have pointed to the obvious: that each problem we've talked about is just a component of the forces that are threatening to bring on a dictatorship. Solving one or two of the problems may help us, but we actually need to solve many problems if we're going to stop going down the road to a dictatorship.

"But we've shown no willingness to solve them. There are small bands of people here and there who see the problems and try to do something, but for ever one who does, there are 30 or 40 who are at home watching TV, and they have no interest in the problems, or they like the way things are going and may have a stake in keeping it this way.

"Almost everything we've talked about here since early this morning is due to the fact that we have surrendered our republican form of government, our personal freedoms, and capitalism to fascism. It's actually over. I truly believe there's really nothing we can do. We could if we *really* wanted to, but we don't. Like the end of a Stephen King horror story, it seems as if escape is right around the corner, but in the last line of the last chapter we discover the horror just goes on and on and on."

"But you've been giving solutions all day to how we can ensure fair trials, how we can end the tyranny of *Executive Orders*, how we can make bureaucracies accountable, how we can regain out lost rights. What can we do about fascism?" Dave asked.

Mac thought long and hard about this.

"Nothing," he finally said.

"Nothing?" Dave asked.

"Think about it," Mac said. "Think about the last 68 years, ever since Roosevelt was elected and we began the descent toward a fascist state. Think about all the changes that have come about, that have eroded our rights, even before 1933, that have occurred in spite of our *Constitution*—which is, incidentally, the only document ever adopted by a nation that put the individual ahead of the state.

"In fact, think about the *Constitution* and how it is the most anti-government document ever written. It was written by the citizens, not some king, philosopher, or a bunch of bureaucrats. It was a document written by free men, some of whom had to wrestle with their consciences because we still were a nation that permitted slavery and not all men were free, that had still not given full freedom to its women, and yet they wrote a document that depended on a nation of free citizens.

"And while you think about that, also think about how all of these changes in our system have come about without any changes to that document. We've lost our rights without altering or repealing the *Bill of Rights*; the federal government's power has expanded without ever amending *Section I, Article 8*, which put restraints on that government. The President now has powers to issue decrees and wage war without consulting either the legislature or the people, and our rights are no longer defended by the people, but are *interpreted* by another branch of the government itself—the courts.

"Almost no one complains about these changes. If you do, you're considered a paranoid nut or an extremist. Even that institution that calls itself the Fifth Estate—the press—no longer holds the feet of politicians and bureaucrats to the fire for trampling on that hallowed document. In fact, they usually encourage it. The press, above all, seems to lead the charge against individual freedoms.

"Look at the stake the bureaucracy, the corporations, and the two major political parties have in at least maintaining the status quo, never mind trampling on our rights even more. Tell me how you realistically think there's a possibility of change for the better?

"Deep down inside I would say there is no solution. We are now a fascist country and things are not ever going to get any better, they'll only get worse."

"You really don't think we can reverse it?" Dave asked.

Mac shook his head. "I've said it before and I'll say it again: someday historians will look back at the late and great United States and wonder how, as we were losing it all, we didn't see it happening. They'll wonder how we let freedom slip through our fingers."

Who's to blame

"So, who's to blame for all of this?" Dave asked.

"We are," Mac said. "We're the boogeymen. We can't really blame the politicians or the bureaucrats. Sometimes they responded to our demands, other times they responded to demands by special interest groups. But all the while we sat at home watching television instead of raising a stink.

"And I'll admit that at other times, the politicians and bureaucrats did things unilaterally to enhance their own powers and, still, we sat home and kept watching our TV programs.

"All we've ever needed to retain our freedoms and ensure a constitutional government, all we ever had to do to have stopped what may one day become the American dictatorship, was to maintain our vigilance. But we didn't. And we don't now.

"On the other hand, maybe fascism isn't so bad. Maybe freedom is overrated. Maybe individual responsibility is an illusion. Maybe all those things we believed about ourselves, those things that we believed set us apart from the rest of the world, as well as from all of the people who have ever lived in history—things like individual freedom, self-reliance, and individual responsibility—are just myths. Maybe it's time for us to join the rest of the world and the rest of history, where rights and freedoms were dispensed by government and bureaucrats. Maybe we should just stop kidding ourselves."

With that, we left the office and headed up to Dave's. I remember that it started raining, yet all day long there hadn't seemed to be a cloud in the sky. Δ

Part IX

The Coming American
Dictatorship Revisited

Mac's back. After a long absence our poker-playing friend from southern California, O.E. MacDougal, walked into the Oregon offices of *Backwoods Home Magazine*.

Poof, and there he was. No phone call, no e-mail, no letter saying he was on his way, no nothin.' We hadn't even heard from him for at least six months. Then, after an almost two-year absence, he just walked through the front door as if he'd stepped out for lunch and had just come back.

For a moment, I didn't even realize who he was. Then, just as it dawned on me, I heard Dave yell from the other side of the office, "Mac!"

Mac smiled faintly as Dave crossed the room and I rose from my desk.

There were handshakes all around and Mac settled into one of the stuffed chairs while Dave and I returned to our desks.

"You look tired," I said.

"Once I left Ventura, I drove nonstop until I got here. Made a couple of stops for gas and another couple to eat."

"No sleep-stops?" I asked.

He shook his head no.

"Wine? A beer?" Dave asked.

Mac looked at the clock. "It's about that time. I'll have whatever you're having."

Dave looked at me as if to ask if I wanted to imbibe and I nodded, and he went to the refrigerator and pulled out a bottle of Concha Y Toro Merlot and popped the cork. He got three glasses from the table near the refrigerator and poured some into each, then passed them around.

We all sat back and there followed some catching up on the news. Mostly it was news about guys Mac and Dave knew way back when.

"What brought you up here?" Dave finally asked.

"I just wanted to get away. Do some fishing. Maybe even do some hiking and see where I may go hunting in the fall."

"Well, we'd be glad to have you come back up," Dave said.

"By the way," he added, "we ran an eight-part series on the stuff you talked about last time you were here. We called it *The Coming American Dictatorship*."

"I saw a few installments," Mac said. He glanced at me and smiled because my byline was on it.

"It was generally well received," Dave said.

"Well, that's nice to hear," Mac responded.

"But we got some letters, I added, "and I spoke with some people who either disagreed with or objected to things you said."

He nodded as if this was something to be expected. "If most people actually agreed with me," he said, "the world would be different."

"If we have some time while you're here, I'd like to do a wrap up," I said.

"Do what?" he asked.

"You know, answer some of the objections people have."

"Like what?" Mac asked.

"Among them some people have said you take the *Constitution* too literally. I've talked with people who say our interpretation of the *Constitution* has to evolve."

Without saying anything, he looked at me funny, as if expecting further explanation.

"You know," I said, "times have changed. They say we need some progress. We can't be solving today's problems with a document that's 200 years old.

"We live in a more dangerous world," I added.

"That's what they're saying?"

"Well, some of them are. They're saying there have never been so many threats to the United States as there are today. The world we live in is more dangerous today than the world of our Founding Fathers."

"Let me give you a different perspective on this," he said:

• In 1776, this country went to war with what was then the world's only superpower.

• We lived on a narrow strip of land along the Atlantic seaboard. For better or worse we had numerous wars, right here on what is today American soil, with the original inhabitants, the Indians.

• We feared the English, the French, and the Spanish. In fact, we feared all of the European powers.

• There were no police forces to speak of.

• The average person only lived into his or her 40s.

• No one knew if the United States would succeed or fail, and virtually every monarchy wanted us to ultimately fail, even if they were temporarily lending us their support during their struggles with each other. The thought of a true democratic republic succeeding, never mind flourishing, was a threat to monarchies everywhere.

"Despite all the dangers, despite living in a dangerous and uncertain world when all of the world's powers wanted democracy and the concept of natural rights to fail, we gave ourselves a relatively weak central government and allowed more rights than any people had ever enjoyed in all of Western history.

"If anything, the world of 225 years ago was a more dangerous and uncertain world, and if there was ever a time with *excuses* to have a strong central government, a time to limit rights, that was it.

"Today we're the world's only superpower. No one can defeat us. Even a nuclear bomb placed in one of our major cities couldn't defeat us. We have never been as secure from foreign forces as we are at this very moment. Yet, many people feel as though now we have to give up our freedoms.

"The irony is today, of all times, is the time when we should be enjoying our rights. Instead, we're talking about how dangerous our rights are."

He hesitated. "I will, however, say one thing: if we live in dangerous times today it's not because of terrorists."

"Then who is it because of?" Dave asked.

"Our own government."

"How can you say that?" I asked.

"It's been that way throughout all of history. The biggest enemy of mankind has not been foreign invaders, or terrorists, or serial killers, or muggers on the street. The most dangerous threat to humanity is almost always our own governments. Hitler killed million of Germans including German Jews. Stalin oversaw the deaths of 20 to 80 million Soviet citizens, Mao another 60 million in China. The Khmer Rouge of Cambodia killed 3 million Cambodians, and who knows how many people Idi Amin killed in Uganda? These aren't isolated cases. All throughout history the primary killer of people has always been their own kind. Governments have been responsible for more deaths to the governed than war or plague. And the people who are most likely to deprive you of your rights and freedoms are your own government. Terrorists aren't going to suspend your rights to free speech, the press, the right to bear arms, or jury trials. Neither are Colombian drug lords nor muggers. It's John Ashcroft, Charles Schumer, George Bush, Tom Daschle, and their kind who will do it.

175

"Now, since 9/11, we've turned to our government for 'safety' and a large number of Americans have expressed their willingness to give up their rights—and my rights, too—for the promise of that safety. We're being told we have to limit our rights and grant more power to politicians, bureaucrats, and the police. We have to give more power to our government. There's a certain amount of irony in that."

"But *we* can trust our government," I said. "It's not like other governments."

"We can't trust an organization that at one time both harbored and fostered slavery and, later, segregation; that abrogated its treaties with the original inhabitants of this continent—the Indians—whenever it chose to; that threw Japanese-Americans in concentration camps for no other reason than their ethnic background; that currently imprisons a larger percentage of its own citizens than any country in the world; that, for the last 30 years, has held the official position of government that property rights of the citizens don't exist...I could go on all day, but it would be senseless. Suffice it to say that this country has a perfectly abominable record and cannot be trusted any more than any other country's government."

"But, compared to other countries, it could be worse," I said.

"Of course it could be worse. But do you think it's not worse because of the innate goodness of our politicians and bureaucrats, or do you think it's because of the restraints our *Constitution* has placed upon them?"

"I'd say, it's the *Constitution* we should trust," Dave said.

I didn't say anything.

Mac said, "We, the American people, should keep in mind that our *Constitution*, when duly followed and enforced, is a *restraint* on our government and a document that *protects* our freedom.

"And it is a mistake to give up any of our rights or to relax our vigilance against our own government, even in light of 9/11."

The Federal Reserve

We sat silently for a few moments. Then I said, "One reader says you don't understand the Federal Reserve, that it's not federally controlled. He said you seem to think it's a part of the federal government, but that it's not. It's a corporation owned by the wealthy. So there's no government solution."

He looked at me curiously.

"I don't care who owns the Federal Reserve. If you go against its edicts, the Rockefellers and Rothschilds are not coming out to your house to visit you. It'll be federal agents. Without Federal backing, the Federal Reserve is powerless. Even those who take that reader's position realize that if the American people would just get control of their government, arguments about the Federal Reserve become moot."

"That makes sense," Dave said.

A universal draft

"We also got an e-mail from a fellow who said...well, here, let me read it to you.

"Sorry, but I cannot agree with John Silveira's position endorsing involuntary servitude (or 'citizens' army' as he puts it) in Part VII of his Coming of the American Dictatorship.

"I agree we need a smaller military, but conscription gives a president a blank check for unlimited manpower in military adventures. Does anyone think if there had been no draft, Presidents Kennedy, Johnson, and Nixon could have pursued the immoral war in Vietnam? For anyone calling oneself a 'libertarian' a military draft should be an anathema! The armed services should be smaller, but they should always be filled with VOLUNTEERS. Conscription is one gateway to tyranny."

"It's signed by a guy named Richard Clark."

Mac nodded. "The war in Vietnam—and you must understand that it wasn't legally a war because no war was declared—was possible because we *only* sent children. If 30, 40, and 50-year-olds had been called up, that war would never have happened.

"Furthermore, the Vietnam War ended *because* of the draft, not in spite of it. Young people took to the streets because they now had a direct stake in it.

"Now, if our military had been like the Swiss, where people up into their 50s are involved, Vietnam wouldn't have even started in the first place.

"The military service I'm talking about, where every man serves, is quite a bit different from drafting 18-year-olds while the vast majority of mature adults stay home.

"And, just for the record, the small volunteer army Mr. Clark is proposing is what we had in the 19th century, and we were in a state of constant war—with the Indians, with the Mexican-American War, the Civil War, and the War with Spain thrown in. Try to imagine how popular warfare would have been if guys from 18 to 55 had to go. Particularly the wars against the Indians.

"On the other hand, if a universal citizen army, such as the Swiss have, was the door that leads to immoral wars, then the Swiss would have been involved in more wars than anyone. They're not involved in any and haven't been for centuries.

"However, having a military made up of volunteers, which is exactly what we have today, hasn't brought about the kind of world Mr. Clark wants, nor has it stopped military adventures by the United States.

"As to involuntary servitude, what Mr. Clark and many other Libertarians want is the ultimate in welfare. Instead of 'give me your money, it's 'go die for me.' I, on the other hand, believe there are certain duties, such as jury duty and responding to a subpoena that, though they could be construed as 'involuntary servitude,' are necessary to the functioning of a free society. And I hold that universal military service is part of our responsibilities if we want a freer society.

He thought another moment. "Furthermore, a professional military is dangerous. I know the Libertarian argument, that we'd get enough volunteers if someone were to invade our country. And it's true. But that's not even close to my point. But if you agree with me that the biggest threat to people since the beginning of civilization has not been wild animals, thugs in the streets, or invading armies, but our own governments, then a professional army must be seen as a danger.

"I believe today's so-called volunteer army will become evermore the tool of foreign adventures and in the future it will be easier for a President to turn the military on the people.

Containing bureaucracy

Again I rummaged around on the mess on my desk, looking for another letter, but I couldn't find it. "Another reader said the idea of making the bureaucracy smaller or even accountable is just wishful thinking on your part and can't be done."

"He's right on the first part, but not the second."

I stopped looking.

"What do mean 'first and second parts?'" Dave asked.

"Well, I think he's right about the part that the idea of the American people getting control of their bureaucracy is just wishful thinking. It's the reason why I ended my talk on a down note. I don't think the American people will actually do anything to change it because they don't realize that the bureaucrats are now part of an unelected permanent government that neither the people nor the Congress exercise much control over. For this reason, the coming American dictatorship may not rest in the hands of one big dictator, but in the tens of thousands of hands of little ones."

"Tens of thousands of bureaucrats," Dave said.

"That's right."

"On the other hand, the part where the reader feels that it can't be stopped is absurd."

"Wait a minute," Dave said. "Do you have examples of things bureaucrats do that we the people, and the Congress in particular, have no control over?" Dave asked.

"Sure. Congress has authorized tax deductions that the IRS has systematically ignored or denied. The Food and Drug Administration has ignored our rights under the *9th* and *10th Amendments* and has assumed suzerainty over our very bodies. And, just recently, Congress has authorized flight crews to carry firearms on commercial airliners, but the Secretary of Transportation, a Clinton appointee, has unilaterally nixed it. Both Congress and the people seem incapable of taking the steps necessary to stopping them. But, in reality, what recourse do the people or the Congress really have?" he asked.

"I don't know, but I think you're going to tell us," Dave said and looked at me.

Mac smiled. "Am I becoming that predictable?" he asked.

"You're very predictable," I said. "But in an unconventional sort of way," I added.

Mac found that funny.

"More wine?" Dave asked.

We all needed more and Dave rose from his chair and started filling each of our glasses.

Mac sat forward. "I'm not sure your remark is very flattering."

"But you *are* kind of predictable," Dave said. "Unfortunately, I've never seen it carry over to the poker table."

"Well, thank heavens for that small blessing," he said and sat back again.

"But, back to your question, if, at the very least, bureaucrats had to allow jury trials—before *randomly* chosen and *fully informed* jurors—and if they had to *prove* guilt, as opposed to having the accused prove innocence, 99 percent of their bureaucratic nonsense would evaporate. It would be too difficult and too expensive to enact and enforce anything but the most sensible regulations. The way it is now, when accused of anything by a bureaucrat, you are too often assumed to be guilty, unless you can *prove* you are innocent."

"Maybe we should just get rid of the bureaucracy," Dave said.

"No, though we have a problem with our bureaucracy, it can be useful, but only when it's under control. We like to think of ourselves as having a representative form of government where elected officials go to the legislatures or Congress, debate the law and exercise the will of the people, all within the framework of the state and federal constitutions with a full eye on our rights. But once it's in the hands of bureaucrats, it's as if the *Constitution* no longer exists. And although we expect the laws that are passed to reflect the will of the people, more and more it isn't the peoples' representatives who are making policy, but unelected bureaucrats. Too often rules and regulations are made that thwart the will of the people, simply because the bureaucrats making the laws can't be voted out, nor can they be recalled."

There was another lull in the conversation as Dave and Mac began talking about fishing and the prospects of hunting in the fall.

What do Libertarians want?

Finally I interrupted. "Hey, I said, "another theme running through some of the letters is that no one knows what Libertarians want. There are people who feel that if Libertarians had their way, nothing would be illegal. There'd wouldn't even be traffic lights or stop signs."

They stopped talking, but Mac didn't say anything. He was looking to me for clarification.

"One even said we've got to draw the line somewhere; otherwise, we'd have people urinating in the street. We'd have people killing each other left and right."

There was a long silence. Finally he asked, "What are you talking about?"

"Another objection to what you said in the series."

"No, I mean, what's this about traffic lights and peeing?"

"It's just that we can't have total freedom or we'd have anarchy and chaos."

He looked around as if making sure I was talking to him. "Where are you going with this?" he asked. He appeared to be genuinely puzzled.

"We've got to have rules," I said.

Finally he said, "You know, I've heard other people make statements like you just made. Things like there being chaos, anarchy, no stop lights when you drive, and who knows what else if Libertarians are elected to office. I've asked other Libertarians if they know anything about this or if this is somewhere in Libertarian doctrine or in the party platform and they're at as much of a loss as I am."

"Then what do you Libertarians want?" I asked.

"If you want a rough idea of what we want, take a look at the *Constitution* including the *Bill of Rights*. Basically, the Libertarians want what's there. And if that's not clear enough, try to think about what Thomas Jefferson, James Madison, or George Mason would want. Do you think when they spoke of freedom they were talking about urinating in the streets or killing each other? Do you think they had urinating in the streets or anarchy when they wrote the *Declaration of Independence* or the first *Ten Amendments* to the *Constitution?*"

He looked at me for a long moment and I realized this wasn't a rhetorical question. He wanted an answer.

"No," I said.

"Well, Libertarians want roughly what those men wanted."

"What do you mean 'roughly'?" Dave asked.

"There are some differences and disagreements among Libertarians just as there were differences among the Founding Fathers."

"What are some of the things Libertarians differ on?" Dave asked.

"There are different positions on abortion, the military, and even the death penalty.

"But there are very few differences concerning freedom of speech, freedom of religion, jury trials, the right to bear arms, property rights, and the like.

"On the other hand, the people who worry about free stop signs and peeing in the street must only be Democrats and Republicans because they're the ones who bring it up when they're talking about Libertarians."

Dave laughed.

"But I'll tell you what," Mac said, "and I think I'm speaking for almost all Libertarians when I say this, we'll make a deal with you: You give us back the *Constitution*, including the political freedoms in the *Bill of Rights*, and abide by the rules spelled out in *Article I, Section 8*, which sets limits on the power of the federal government, and *Article V*, which explains how the *Constitution* is to be amended—and it's not by reinterpretation—and we'll give you *all* the stop signs you want. We'll put them every 50 feet, if that's what you really want. And if the Democrats and Republicans want to pee in the streets, go ahead. I can assure you the Libertarians don't really want to join you—at least the ones I know won't. But if you guarantee us the right to do what we want with our own bodies, to express ourselves the way we want to, to have fair trials before juries that aren't handpicked by either the state or defense attorney—but especially by the state—we'll allow you to pee anywhere you want. And, if this is what it takes, we'll even pee with you."

I thought Dave was going to fall out of his chair.

"What about abortion?" I asked.

"That's a genuine debate among Libertarians. There are those who feel abortion is okay because they focus on the rights of the woman. But there are also those who feel that a human's civil rights begin with conception."

"But at conception it's not human yet. It's just tissue."

He shrugged. "You're playing a semantics game here," he said.

183

"What do you mean?" he asked.

"If a woman randomly gave birth to fish, dogs, and ponies, as well as human babies, I'd say you have a point calling it just tissue. But they don't. So it's hard to take the 'just tissue' arguments seriously.

"The question among Libertarians is: When do you want to confer civil rights? Do you choose to do that when the fetus is viable, do you wait until the child reaches the first grade? If you wait until the first grade you practice something akin to infanticide, and there are societies that condone infanticide. But pick a point when someone has rights. Just don't use the 'just tissue' argument because I don't understand it and I don't buy into it."

"This sounds like the same argument that exists between the pro-choice advocates and the pro-lifers," Dave said, "except that they're arguing about when life really begins, or when there's a soul, or whatever."

"Yes. But Libertarians generally confine it to a political argument," Mac replied.

"So Libertarians don't just march in lockstep," I said. "They actually do disagree among themselves."

"The ones I know do," Mac said.

Following orders

We sat there while Dave and Mac stared at me. They knew I wasn't going to let them go on with more pleasant thoughts of hunting and fishing until I asked all of my questions.

I thought about other objections I'd heard.

"Yeah," I said, "another opinion I've heard raised by several people is that there is far too much worry about 'our rights.' These people feel that if you just do what you're supposed to do, you know, obey all the laws and regulations, and if you've got nothing to hide, you don't have to worry about your rights."

"They're right," Mac responded.

"They are?"

184

"Sure. But it's not only true here, it's true in every country. 'Toe the line and you won't get in trouble.' Think about it: If the women in Afghanistan, living under the Taliban, just wore their burkas as they were told to, refrained from driving, and stopped trying to get an education they would have been all right.

"If students in South Korea and China hadn't insisted on demonstrating for what they called human rights, they wouldn't have been beaten by the police. If people hadn't pressed for freedom and reforms in Chile in the '80s, they wouldn't have 'disappeared,' and if slaves had just toed the line in the 1800s they wouldn't have been beaten or hung and there wouldn't have been a War Between the States.

"In fact, if blacks in the American South hadn't insisted on equality in the 60s, and if they hadn't staged their sit-ins, civil rights marches, and access-to-the-ballot-box demonstrations they wouldn't have been arrested, thrown in jail, or killed."

He waited for a response, but I didn't say anything.

"You see, all you're really saying is, 'Do as you're told and you'll be all right.' And, John, it's true. If we just let the government use all of the tools available to it, even if its actions contravene the *Constitution* and the *Bill of Rights*, you'll be okay as long as you don't complain and go along with the program. And if you don't stand up for the people who do protest, and just let the authorities deal with them as they see fit, you'll still be okay. In World War II the Nazis may have put Jews in ovens, but if you were Lutheran or Catholic and *didn't* complain about it, nothing happened to you because you were doing as you were told and obeying the law."

"But that stuff is different. What I mean is that if you aren't doing anything *wrong*, you have nothing to fear," I said.

"And what do you mean by 'wrong?' Does the state determine what's wrong? If so, then if freedom of religion is deemed illegal, or free speech goes away, or if we dispense with trial by jury, then as long as you don't complain and you do what the government tells you, and you don't stand up for people who are persecuted for demanding these freedoms, then you're okay.

"That's a prescription for total tyranny, especially as the bureaucrats, politicians, and special interests get bolder. They already deny us the right to carry arms without permits, they seize our property with civil forfeiture laws—without even charging us with crimes, they even deny us the right to do with our own bodies as we please with their medical laws and laws about consensual sex. They are making more and more things 'wrong' all the time. And worse yet is that a lot of the things they find wrong are what we call consensual crimes, like smoking pot or playing poker—although the states ignore their own lotteries. I can't even enter into certain contracts with another consenting adult for medical aid, legal advice, or to have a rumpus room put on my house unless the state blesses it."

"You're saying there's no virtue in just following orders," Dave said.

"No, there isn't."

"What do we do?" Dave asked.

The solution

"You know, all the time I spoke before, you kept asking for solutions," Mac said. "Here's the solution to everything:

"If Americans really want their rights and constitutional government back, the first thing they'll do is regain control of the jury system—*our* jury system—and most of the silly laws in this country will just evaporate away.

"Remember, it's not the government's jury system, it's ours. And it's not there for the benefit of the government nor of lawyers, but for us. We've let the entire jury system be subverted by lawyers, judges, bureaucrats, and politicians.

"But if Americans aren't willing to regain possession of the jury system by making themselves aware of jury nullification and demanding random juries, then how are we going to regain possession of more difficult aspects of our government? We're not."

"But there are others who think that you're wrong here," I said. "They feel that in the United States it's senseless to complain about the government because here the people *are* the government."

He laughed.

"I don't know who first came up with that saying," he said. "It's an Orwellian concept and it's not true either in fact or in theory. If it were true, the *Constitution* wouldn't be written the way it is. The *Constitution* is very clear that there are the people, the states, and the federal government. It is also pretty explicit in how it puts limits on the federal government—not that anyone pays much attention to that anymore.

"And, one other thing, this aspect of the *Constitution*—its purpose of being a restraint on government—should be taught in the schools. That would be another part of the solution, to start showing people what the *Constitution* actually says, right from the time we're kids."

Dave said, "Everything you're saying still comes back to the fact that things aren't going to get better unless the American people actually get off their collective butts and do something, and..."

Mac and I sat there for a moment waiting for him to finish..

"...*and* what?" I finally asked.

"...and, Mac, you don't expect us to do it, do you?"

"No, I don't."

"Why?"

"We're different, now. Different from the guys who founded this country. You know, if you ever get around to reading about the actual events that led up to the Revolutionary War, the things that led farmers to take to the heights of Bunker Hill to fight the British and which eventually led to the *Declaration of Independence* and the War itself, they will seem, by today's standards, to be almost nothing. It was just a few unfair taxes, curtailment of some of our natural rights, and an unresponsive government. Americans today bear oppression hundreds of times worse with nary a protest. We've gotten used to it. And as we become accustomed to the abuses and incursions into our rights, what may be outrageous and unbearable today will become the norm tomorrow and new incursions will be made.

"And anyone who complains, or points out that our federal government is *illegal* by the terms of the *Constitution*, is stereotyped and branded as a right wing extremist, a carper, or a complainer."

"And it is for those very reasons that you think an American dictatorship is inevitable," Dave said.

"That's right. I've come to think that subservience of the people to kings, bureaucrats, etc. is the natural state of mankind and that the concept that the people have individual rights is just so much rhetoric, and no one has ever said anything to make me think differently."

"So, you stand by everything you said that I put in the series I wrote," I said.

He thought several seconds, and then he nodded. "I do."

"Then that answers the last objection I remember," I said, "and that was why the series ended on a down note."

"Freedom is always within our grasp," he said. "The question is, will we reach for it? And I don't think, as a people, we will."

There was another silence.

"So, what do you want to hunt?" I asked.

"Upland birds, water fowl, maybe some deer."

"Let's start making plans," Dave said. ∆

Part X

How special interests are writing our laws and destroying America

It had been a long time since we'd seen him, but when I heard the commotion in the outer offices I took a guess as to who had arrived. Dave Duffy yelled, "Mac! How are you doing?" It was O.E. MacDougal, our poker-playing friend, visiting the magazine after a lengthy hiatus.

"Come this way," Dave said enthusiastically. "We're working on the new issue. What brings you up here?"

"Winter steelhead and spring salmon," Mac said as he entered the editorial office.

"Gonna fish the Rogue?" I asked.

He nodded and said, "How are ya, John?"

"Fine," I replied.

The Rogue River runs into the Pacific about a mile north of us here in Gold Beach where *Backwoods Home Magazine* is located, and it's one of Mac's favorite places to fish.

"Who you going out with?" Dave asked.

"You, of course," Mac said. "in your new boat. Any suggestions for a guide?"

"Dave Anderson," Dave said. "I just wrote a story about him. Very knowledgeable. He's going to do a column for the magazine."

"Great!" he said.

With that they both looked at me.

"Yeah," I said. "I'll go, too."

As Dave settled back into the routine of deadline, Mac pulled up a chair beside my desk and asked, "What are you writing about this issue, John?"

"I'm doing an article on the guy who invented the safety pin."

"Walter Hunt? Yeah, he's an interesting character," Mac said.

"Who?" I asked.

Mac looked at me kind of skeptically. "Walter Hunt, the guy you're writing about. The guy who invented the safety pin."

I hesitated. "Is this a joke?"

"No, he invented it. Did you think someone else did?"

"Actually, I was the one who was joking," I admitted. "I said I'm writing about the guy who invented the safety pin because I can't think of anything to write about. I didn't know anyone had actually invented the safety pin. I didn't think of it as something that actually had to be invented."

"Yeah. He invented and patented it in the early 1800s." Mac said. "Truth be known, Hunt is worth writing about. He was an interesting guy."

"Oh," I said.

Dave interrupted us and asked, "Anderson wants to know when you want to go?"

"The sooner the better," Mac replied.

"Tomorrow okay, Mac?"

"Tomorrow's great."

I nodded in agreement.

"Have you been fishing lately?" Mac asked Dave as he hung up.

"Yeah. Anderson and I have gone out several times. We're trying to make a video for the digital issue."

"Digital issue?" Mac asked, surprised.

As they started talking about fishing and the magazine, I furtively went out online and checked to see if Mac had been pulling my leg. But, with a little Googling, there he was, Walter Hunt, and he had, indeed, invented the safety pin. And just as Mac said, he was an interesting character because he had invented several things including a forerunner of the Winchester repeating rifle, road sweeping machinery, ice plows, an early sewing machine, and a host of other things. He had patents for many inventions.

"What do you think about what's happening in Washington nowadays?" Dave asked.

"I don't like what's going on," Mac said.

With that, I closed the site. I wanted to hear what Mac had to say. I'd read more about Hunt later.

Who writes our laws?

"What do you think of the bills coming out of Congress?" Dave asked.

"Not much. Each time I see one, I wonder who actually wrote it."

"What do you mean," I asked. "It's a congressman, isn't it? Or someone on his staff?"

"Often, it's not," he said.

"What do you mean? If congressmen don't write the laws, who does?" I said.

"It's not always the lawmakers."

When I gave him a quizzical look, he said, "You don't think Congressmen or even their staffs have vast stores of wisdom they tap to take care of us, do you? Not to say that they never do. But there are thousands and thousands of bills introduced every year. Even with 535 people between the two Chambers, they can't write them all. In fact, they don't write many of them, at all."

"Then who does?" I asked.

"Not only congressmen, but state legislators are often spoon-fed the laws they introduce by special interest groups. These can be

191

corporations or groups of corporations, advocacy groups, and whatnot. Even bureaucratic departments are often handed the substance of the regulations they invoke by special interest groups."

"They can just be handed bills?" I asked.

"Sure. They even have or hire lawyers that write them up."

He must have seen the confusion on my face because he added, "Not all of them come that way, but quite a few."

"What are the other ways?" I asked.

"There are several avenues a potential law can go down at both federal and state levels. For instance, your congressmen—or your state legislators—might actually listen to their constituents' desires and formulate legislation based on them. But I think this is becoming the least likely way for a law to be introduced.

"Another way is the congressmen or legislators follow the polls, or their staffs do and tell them what the popular position is on this or that. I think we've seen a lot of this in the past and will continue to see it in the future."

"Well, that makes sense," I said. "They're supposed to do what the majority wants."

Mac shook his head. "It's what they often do, but it's not what they're supposed to do. They're supposed to do what's right, not what's popular. By that I mean that sometimes the majority wants laws that violate the minority's rights. With the form of government we have, our legislators are supposed to follow constitutional guidelines."

"That makes more sense," I said.

"Along those same lines, that is, of trying to find what's popular, congressmen often cannot resist grandstanding when there's something big in the news. The steroids problem in baseball is an example. But I can't think of many things dumber than congressional hearings about what baseball players are doing with their own bodies.

"Instead of addressing the looming economic disaster that is heading our way, they were holding hearings on how private businesses like baseball teams, and private individuals, such as the players, conduct their lives. But that's for the teams and the players to sort out; it's not a congressional problem."

I nodded.

"Another example is that woman in California who gave birth to eight babies after embryo implants. The press even has a name for her — 'Octomom.'

"Criticizing her has become all the rage, and perhaps justly so. But in several states, lawmakers have seen fit to introduce bills to limit the number of embryos a woman can have implanted. What an incredible waste of public resources. If those legislators have nothing better to do, or can't think of real problems to confront, they should give up their seats and and let someone else handle the job."

"But isn't a woman having that many kids a problem?" I asked.

"Is it?"

"I think so. The taxpayers in California are the ones who are going to have to pick up the tab," I said.

"So?"

For the first time, I thought Mac was being unreasonable. I said, "Supporting those eight kids along with the other six she has is going to take a lot of money."

"Okay," he said. "I'll grant you that eight more kids are going to be more of a burden on the taxpayer. But if that's a problem, why aren't we talking about the real problem?"

"What's that?" I asked.

"The thousands and thousands of single mothers with one, two, or more children being supported by taxpayers. There are hundreds of thousands of such children. Isn't that the real problem?

"The way I see it, when one woman has eight kids taxpayers must support, the people, the press, and the legislators are outraged. But when a million women have one, two, or three kids each that taxpayers must support, no one says a word. They silently support them with their taxes."

"What you're saying," Dave interrupted, "is that the legislators are grandstanding over something that's caught the public's fancy while ignoring the core problems we're facing."

"That's exactly what they're doing."

"And," Dave continued, "often they're not going to address real issues, like all the moms having these kids, because not only are they not popular issues, but it's become politically incorrect to talk about them."

Dave paused and thought a second. "In fact, in today's political climate it can be political suicide."

"That's what I'm saying, and that's the kind of people we have serving us," Mac said. "We have legislators who would rather play it safe and take up only safe causes rather than face real problems. Squaring off against someone like Octomom can get a legislator's name on television, radio, and the Internet, but it doesn't solve the underlying problem."

Mac continued, "But let's take a more pressing issue. It's not going to make the news if a congressman wants to hold hearings on farm subsidies, a subject that is costing the taxpayers billions and billions of dollars every year, but gets little press. Voters don't think about it and they don't discuss it, though those subsidies have been taking money out of our pockets at an obscene rate for decades—more money than 10,000 Octomoms would."

"So you're saying a lot of laws exist just because they're part of what's popular in the news, and we're not paying attention to what's actually important," Dave said.

"I'd say so."

When there was a pause, Mac continued, "Another way laws can be submitted to the Congress is by the President," Mac continued. "This is how the PATRIOT Act came about."

"Is that bad, having the President propose legislation?" I asked.

"Not at all. The President should be able to propose legislation if he thinks he needs it to be able to do his job. But the Congress doesn't have to accept legislation proposed by the President. The problem with the PATRIOT Act, proposed by President Bush, is that when it got to Congress, it didn't undergo debate and it didn't undergo public scrutiny. It wasn't even read by the overwhelming majority of the men and women we sent to Congress. Yet, they overwhelmingly voted for it."

"Without knowing what it said," Dave added.

Mac nodded. "And it's probably the single worst piece of legislation in our lifetimes.

"But, here's another way for bills to get introduced, and I find it more disturbing than the ways I just mentioned. Bills come into Congress, more often than you think, straight from special interest groups."

"That's what you said earlier," I said.

He nodded. "Groups with money and influence approach a congressman and hand him a bill just as they want it drawn up. And this doesn't just happen in Washington, it happens in state capitols all the time.

"Special interests, from General Motors to the Sierra Club to the AFL-CIO, have easier access to your congressman's ear. They also are more visible contributors to their campaigns. Their lobbyists also meet your congressman at the cocktail parties around the capitol."

"They become familiar," Dave said.

"Yeah. But if you or I want to suggest legislation, we can barely get our congressman's ear. We're lucky if we even get our congressman's staff to send back a form letter saying 'thank you.'

"Worse, the special interests often have teams of lawyers who write up and hand your congressman the legislation, in the vague legalese it's apparently supposed to be written in, so your congressman doesn't have to pay his staff to do it.

"But there's something even worse: These special interests can also approach a bureaucrat and hand him or her a piece of legislation."

"Why's that worse than giving it to a congressman?" Dave asked.

"Let's compare what happens when your congressman is handed proposed legislation to when a bureaucrat is handed it.

"In the first case, when your congressman gets a proposed bill from a special interest group, he still has to introduce it into whichever of the congressional chambers he's in. He tries to get cosponsors. A bill without cosponsors is hard to get passed. Next, he has to get it out of committee, to the floor, to get it voted on. If it was introduced into the House, and it passes on a House vote, it has to go to the Senate and, if both the House and Senate agree on it, it still has to be signed into law by the President. And, if the President vetoes it, it may die, unless Congress overrides the President's veto with a vote of at least two-thirds of each Chamber.

"And if a senator wants to introduce a bill, it has to undergo the same process and the Senate has to get the House to agree before it's sent on to the President. The biggest difference is that any bill that involves money cannot originate in the Senate—not to say that's never happened, but we'll talk about that, later.

"I'm sure you learned the whole process of how laws are passed in grade school. Maybe you don't remember it."

"I missed school that day," I said, and Mac smiled.

"Most people missed school that day," he said.

"It's sounds like an arduous process," Dave said.

"It is," Mac said. "And it's a fairly decent process because it guarantees—or is supposed to guarantee—the bill will be debated and considered by those who represent us in Congress or, if it's at the state level, in the state legislature. Of course, sometimes it doesn't work out that way, as with PATRIOT Act..."

"...which wasn't debated and they didn't even read it," Dave said finishing Mac's sentence.

"That's right."

"But, in the second case, a special interest circumvents the legislative process and goes right to a bureaucrat, and that's not good."

"Why?" Dave asked.

"Do you know how the bureaucracy works?" he asked.

Neither of us answered.

"Okay," Mac said. "The various departments of our government were empowered with certain regulatory powers by Congress when they were created, and the departments use those powers to make rules and regulations so they can do their jobs. Those rules and regulations become the law of the land just as sure as any statutory laws do. But they become law with no debate."

Dave waved his arms. "Okay, stop," he said. "Let's slow down. Can you give us examples of bills that have been introduced each way so we have something real to deal with? Give us an example of one that could be proposed to Congress or a state legislature, then give us another that could become law by way of a bureaucratic department? I want real-world examples so I can understand what you're talking about."

"Sure. I can come up with two examples that are of interest not only to you, but to your readers because they're going to affect them in a negative way if they're enacted. Both are examples of things written by special interest groups.

"The first is the Ammunition Accountability Act. I see you guys had it as the subject of the Last Word in the last issue (See BHM Issue 116, March/April 2009.). If you look at the dozen and a half or so states where it's been introduced, you'll see it had pretty much the same wording in each state. That's because..."

"It was drawn up by the same people and handed to legislators in each of those states," Dave interrupted.

"That's right. The bill wasn't thought up by some legislators themselves who saw a problem. The Ammunition Accountability Act was drafted by and given to handpicked legislators in each of those states by gun control groups that were big campaign contributors, and by the people who hope to profit from making the equipment to stamp all the billions of rounds of ammunition that will be produced. But those groups have tried to distance themselves from the Act because they want to disguise it as a crime control bill rather than the gun control bill it really is.

"The good news is gun owners saw through it right away, and it's gone down to defeat in state after state. It got defeated in those states because it was debated by legislators, and voters contacted their legislators with their concerns.

"And, of course, the reason for that is that there's something like 70 million gun owners in this country and even the dumbest state legislator realizes irate gun owners can swing an election," Mac said.

"Is there an example of something that went straight to the bureaucrats, that our readers would be interested in?" Dave asked.

"Yes. The National Animal Identification System (NAIS). It's a scheme...yeah, 'scheme' is a good word here...for registering animals."

"What is it about?" Dave asked.

"Its stated purpose is to keep track of all agricultural animals: cattle, pigs, sheep, goats, horses, chickens, turkeys...You get the idea. If it's an agricultural animal, you're going to have to register it, put chip implants in it that can be tracked, send your information to a government computer, report every time you move it, sell it, slaughter it...the whole shebang."

"It sounds pretty innocuous," I said.

"It's not!" Mac said.

"Who wrote it?" Dave asked.

"The bill was drafted by the National Institute of Animal Agriculture (NIAA) which is not a governmental agency, but a 'private' organization made up of various chemical and pharmaceutical corporations, agribusinesses, and the corporations who hope to profit from manufacturing the tracking equipment."

"How many chickens do you have up at your house?" he asked Dave.

198

"A dozen," Dave said.

"So you'd need 12 chips, one for each chicken. Each chicken would have to be registered with the government."

"Wow!" I said. Then one of those egg farms with 100,000 chicks would would need 100,000 chips. That'll cause food prices to go up."

"Actually, they won't. They'd only need one."

"One?" I asked.

"Yes."

"How can they justify just one chip for 100,000 hens while Dave has to get a different one for each of his 12 chickens?"

"Keep in mind, it wasn't written by Congress, and it wasn't even written by the USDA, the department that's trying to implement it."

"You said it was written by NIAA, a private group," Dave said.

"Yes. But you and your readers are going to have to live under it and abide by its rules if it's enacted."

Dave asked, "How can they justify one chip for each of my birds while they only need one for their 100,000 chickens...?"

"Their rationale is that their 100,000 hens are a single unit. That's how those businesses operate. On the other hand, your chickens are seen as separate units. You could give one away, sell another to a neighbor, another two may run away, and you may even get more of them. The agribusinesses..."

"The one's writing the regulation..." Dave interrupted again.

"That's right, the agribusinesses, pharmaceutical companies, the other companies that hope to manufacture the chips, and the companies that hope to provide contractor support to the USDA, reason that the egg farms get 100,000 hens all at once, they're all housed together, and when their laying days are over, they finally all get slaughtered together. So, they argue—and rather forcefully at that—their 100,000 hens are a single unit and one chip is enough to track them all. The same goes for herds of cattle, hogs, sheep, etc., that are owned by big business. Your 12 chickens may not stay together so they want you to report every movement or event of each of them—including if you decide to make soup out of one of them—to the government within 48 hours. Otherwise, you're breaking the law and, for that, there are fines and penalties, all suggested by the NIAA."

"This sounds like something they'd have done in Nazi Germany or the Soviet Union," I said.

Mac laughed. "Got a kid in 4H with a pig? It's got to be registered. Your kid wants to take it to Fair and enter it in competition? A report has to be filed with the government. Then your kid wants to sell it at auction? Got to file the transaction with the government.

"Got a kid with a horse she wants to ride in a parade. Gotta let the government know that you're moving it."

"What if they don't know if you've got animals?" I asked. "It seems to me that a lot of people would hide what they're doing rather than comply."

"If you don't register your premises..."

"Register your premises?" Dave asked.

"Oh, I didn't say that? Yes, you're going to have to register your house just to have your chickens. And if you don't register them and pay your fees to comply, you'll get in trouble if you have to pay a visit to a veterinarian, because the veterinarian will legally be obligated to turn you in."

Mac added: "And if you don't report every move or exchange of your animals and every egg you hatch to a bureaucrat within 48 hours, you're also breaking the law."

"Exactly what are the penalties?" I asked.

"The USDA doesn't want to discuss them just now," Mac replied.

There was a long pause.

"They're trying to get this enacted without letting us know what the penalties for noncompliance are?" I asked.

"Well, you can guess what they might be. The way government invariably operates you can assume it will be a mixture of fines, property seizures, and jail time."

"What's the excuse...intention...reason for all this?" I asked grasping for words. "What do we need it for?"

"It's supposed to put in place a way of tracking animal diseases in our food system."

Dave and I looked at each other. "Are there diseases running rampant through the animals we raise that have to be tracked?" I asked.

"No," Mac said.

"Then what will it actually do?" I asked.

"It sounds to me like something to expand bureaucratic power and benefit big business by driving small businesses and family farms out of business," Dave said.

"That is a problem," Mac said. "But the NAIS is also about the Japanese."

"The Japanese?" Dave asked incredulously. "How do they figure in?"

"In the past, Japan has been the biggest foreign market for American beef, worth about $1.5 billion a year in trade. When we had the mad cow disease scare a few years ago, the market for American beef in Japan dried up. American cattle producers lost that $1.5-billion-a-year business. It's become part of the push to get NAIS through. It is very much about convincing the Japanese our beef is safe so American beef producers can get back into that market."

"While, at the same time, making it harder for small farmers and family farms and even forcing some small American businesses and family farms out of business." Dave said.

"That's about the size of it."

"Is anyone opposing NAIS?" I asked.

"Most people don't even know it's out there. But it is opposed by small farmers including the Amish who reject modern technology on religious grounds, by consumer groups, and by freedom advocates. It's found opposition among both liberals and conservatives. And it's opposed by many on constitutional grounds."

"Like what?" I asked.

"Opponents say the NAIS violates the *First, Fourth, Fifth, Ninth, Tenth*, and *Fourteenth Amendments*, as well as *Article I, Section 8* of the *Constitution*. There's organized opposition in all 50 states."

"Are you kidding?" I asked.

"No."

"So by going straight to the bureaucrats, NIAA is attempting an end run around the democratic process and avoiding public debate and scrutiny," Dave said.

"And they may well succeed," Mac said. "The USDA has now got the funding to implement it and, at the moment, there doesn't appear to be enough voices in Congress to stop it."

Dave sat there shaking his head.

"What's the trouble, Dave?" Mac asked.

"These are regulations that are liable to become, as the *Constitution* says, 'the law of the land.' But they're not being written with regard to our rights, they're not being debated in Congress. They're being written by faceless corporations and they're going to be implemented by faceless bureaucrats."

"That's why bills and regulations being handed to politicians and bureaucrats, but especially to bureaucrats, bother me so much," Mac said.

"And," he added, "it's all part of the broader picture we've talked about before. It's more laws and more penalties.

"As it is, the United States is already the most regulated country in history. We have more laws than any other country has ever had in history. No American can go through a single day without breaking some laws. And you know quite a few farm families are going to violate the NAIS rules unintentionally when they butcher a chicken for Sunday dinner or give a few laying hens to a new neighbor and forget to report them."

The solution

"What's the solution?" Dave asked.

"Well, we have two things here," Mac said. "One is what to do about the NAIS, specifically. The other is the general question of what to do about regulations written by special interest groups and handed to a bureaucrat, as the NAIS has been."

"The first part of your question is tough to answer because the NAIS has already gone so far down the line. It's already being implemented, it's already being funded."

"Would you recommend noncompliance?" I asked.

"Only if it were done in an organized fashion, like the civil rights protests and sit-ins in the '60s. But I don't see any organizations doing that yet. And you have to keep in mind that had sit-ins of the '60s not been done as a concerted effort, with many people involved and the press as a sympathetic witness, the sit-in demonstrators would simply have been arrested and gone to jail and would not have accomplished anything. Unless there is an organized resistance to the implementation of NAIS that can bring public attention to it, I would not advise anybody to try to resist or duck it alone.

"For the time being, the best thing you can do is to inform yourself about it, then write a letter to your Representative in Congress and one to your Senator. An avalanche of letters has the chance to get a congressman's attention. And, specifically, you should mention that there is an online Federal Registry (http://www.regulations.gov/fdmspublic/component/main?main=DocketDetail&d=APHIS-2007-0096) where some 5,000 comments have been posted concerning the NAIS, most of which oppose it, and they should require the USDA to respond to them."

"What will that accomplish?" Dave asked.

"Tell your congressman that what we need is a moratorium on it so we can have a public debate concerning it, so we can understand the ramifications of what NAIS will do. Tell him or her that he should understand that we're entitled to it since it's going to affect us all.

"Next, go where the money is. For example, the hatcheries. Some of them sell millions of baby chicks every year. Under the NAIS they'll be required to band or implant chips in the millions of chickens they sell every year. Many of those suppliers are already on our side.

"Other companies, those that sell farm equipment and animal feeds, should be reminded they're going to lose business if small producers and family farms have to stop raising animals because the NAIS makes it impractical or unprofitable.

"Support efforts in your state to prohibit the registering of animals. Most states have introduced bills to prohibit it, but only one, Arizona, has passed one. However, the problem here is that, if NAIS passes into regulation on the federal level, it will trump any state resistance.

"I'd also say that, for now, while compliance is 'voluntary,' if you need to take an animal to the vet—I'm not talking about dogs and cats, but agricultural animals—or have the vet visit your farm, tell him or her not to enter you into the system. It is when the so-called voluntary compliance reaches a certain critical mass that the USDA will claim they have the green light to go ahead with the NAIS. Don't let them make you become a part of that critical mass.

"As to the general part of the problem, we have a lot of laws and regulations whose origins are with special interest groups, not with the people or with our representatives. And very often with those laws and regulations, our rights take a back seat."

"And because of that," Dave said, "we have people other than our lawmakers—our Representatives and Senators, the people who are supposed to be speaking for us—writing our laws."

"Sometimes," Mac said, "they're corporations, and sometimes they're advocacy groups. But they are writing laws that are filled with penalties, often work against our freedoms, often are unconstitutional, and in the worst cases, they don't even go through our legislators who are supposed to debate them for us. They're not even signed into law by the President. They just become rules we have to obey."

"And the solution to that...?" Dave asked.

"The real solution is that we've got to make Congress realize that when bureaucrats want to create new regulations, they should have to send them to Congress so they undergo the legislative process with input by the Congress, the President, and the people before we have to live under them."

"Is that ever going to happen?" Dave asked.

"It will if we make a stink about it. Otherwise, we'll get the government we deserve."

"But wouldn't that make government less efficient?" I asked.

"And the downside of that is...?" Mac asked and Dave laughed. Δ

Part XI

The Tenth Amendment Movement

O.E. MacDougal, Dave Duffy's poker-playing buddy from Southern California, had come to town to fish the Rogue, a river that runs 215 miles from the heels of Crater Lake through forest and rapids until it reaches the small town of Gold Beach, Oregon, a turbulent outlet to the Pacific but a major inlet for king salmon.

This morning Mac didn't look like he was in a hurry to get out to the river. He sat drinking his third cup of coffee, chatting with us about the state of the economy, what makes women beautiful, and the best recipes for salmon. He's passionate about the last.

When there was a major lull in the conversation, Dave commented, "We've gotten some mail about the Tenth Amendment Movement. But, other than the letters, I haven't heard much about it. Are you familiar with it, Mac?"

"Sure," Mac said. "It's an attempt by the states to stop the expansion of the powers of the federal government and to reassert the original intent of the clauses in *Article I, Section 8*, and the *Ninth* and *Tenth Amendments* of the *Constitution*."

"What do you mean by 'original intent?'" Dave asked.

"The *Constitution* allows certain powers to the federal government, but leaves all other governmental authority with the states. And for about the first 150 years that's pretty much the way things were. But that's not what's happening now.

"Today, many people feel as though the federal government has assumed too much power. The Tenth Amendment Movement is simply an attempt by the states to restore the balance of power they feel the Founding Fathers intended when they wrote the *Constitution*. Sometimes it's called the State Sovereignty Movement."

"Restoring the balance of power? That's all it's about?" I asked.

"Pretty much."

"Why is there no discussion in the mainstream media?" Dave asked. "Especially in the news."

"Because it's the mainstream media!" Mac said. "It's easier to ignore an issue you don't like; the alternative media, especially on the Internet, is abuzz with Tenth Amendment Movement discussion."

I chimed in, "There are those who claim the Tenth Amendment Movement could lead to secession by the states and even to the disbanding of the United States."

Mac smiled. "That implies that by going back to the way the United States was 70 years ago, and reasserting the original balance of power between the states, the people, and the federal government, we're going to cause the country to dissolve. It's a phony claim, but some of the movement's opponents want you to see it that way."

"Why?" I asked.

"One way to counter anything is to misrepresent it."

"What do you mean?"

"Instead of fighting against the real issue — in this case, restoring the balance of power between the people, the states, and the federal government — it's easier to argue against the manufactured issue, and the manufactured issue is the threat of secession."

> ## Amendment X
>
> The powers not delegated to the United States by the Constitution, nor prohibited by it to the States, are reserved to the States respectively, or to the people.

208

"If it really were about secession," Dave said, turning to me, "the media would be all over it. Secession is too good a story to pass up."

"That's actually a good point," Mac said.

"But why do we need a 'movement' like this, anyway?" I asked.

Mac paused and his eyes went to the ceiling for a moment as if looking for some words.

"Let's go back to the beginning of the story—the beginning of this country, that is. Many of the Founding Fathers didn't want a powerful centralized government. So, what they did, in 1787, when they drafted the *Constitution*, was to define and limit the federal government's powers in *Article I, Section 8*. And a few years later, with the adoption of the *Ninth* and *Tenth Amendments*, they felt they had further clarified the subject.

Preamble to the Bill of Rights

Congress of the United States begun and held at the City of New-York, on Wednesday the fourth of March, one thousand seven hundred and eighty nine.

The Conventions of a number of the States, having at the time of their adopting the Constitution, expressed a desire, in order to prevent misconstruction or abuse of its powers, that further declaratory and restrictive clauses should be added: And as extending the ground of public confidence in the Government, will best ensure the beneficent ends of its institution.

Resolved by the Senate and House of Representatives of the United States of America, in Congress assembled, two thirds of both Houses concurring, that the following Articles be proposed to the Legislatures of the several States as amendments to the Constitution of the United States, all, or any of which articles, when ratified by three fourths of the said Legislatures, to be valid to all intents and purposes, as part of the said Constitution; viz.

Articles in addition to, and Amendment of the Constitution of the United States of America, proposed by Congress, and ratified by the Legislatures of the several States, pursuant to the fifth Article of the original Constitution.

(Emphasis by me, JE Silveira)

"But the problem is that, despite the restraints placed in the *Constitution*, right from the earliest days of the Republic, the federal government has tried to expand its power. But it rarely got very far doing it until the 'big government' era that started with the Great Depression."

"What happened then?" I asked.

"First, President Franklin Delano Roosevelt, then the Congress, and finally, after threats from FDR, the courts began to reinterpret the *Constitution*."

"What kind of reinterpretation?" Dave asked.

"Those advocating a powerful centralized government began to circumvent the restrictions placed on the federal government by putting a new spin on what is called the commerce clause and coupled it with the necessary and proper clause."

Mac got out of his seat and retrieved Dave's almanac from the shelf near him.

"What are those?" Dave asked.

"I knew you were going to ask that," Mac said as he held the book up. Then he sat back down and leafed through its pages.

"Both the commerce clause and the necessary and proper clause are part of *Article I, Section 8*, which is that part of the *Constitution* that lists the powers the federal government is allowed to exercise," he said.

"The commerce clause states..." and he began to read from the almanac "...that Congress shall have the power to..." and he ran his finger down the page, "To regulate Commerce with foreign Nations, and among the several States, and with the Indian Tribes."

"The original intent of the commerce clause was to regulate trade among the states and to ensure there would be no duties or tariffs between them. The rest of the clause was meant to regulate trade with foreign countries and the Indian tribes. However, those parts of it don't concern us here. So, for the first 150 years, that's how the clause was used. But for the last 70 years the part that pertains to the states has

210

been reinterpreted and used in conjunction with the necessary and proper clause to mean the federal government can regulate almost anything that takes place between states no matter how remote.

"And the necessary and proper clause...?" Dave asked.

"That clause states that Congress has the power 'To make all Laws which shall be necessary and proper for carrying into Execution the foregoing Powers, and all other Powers vested by this *Constitution* in the Government of the United States, or in any Department or Officer thereof.'"

"That sounds reasonable," Dave said.

"Some of the Founders, guys like Jefferson, were afraid the clause was granting the federal government unbridled power."

"Does it?" I asked.

"According to Alexander Hamilton, another of the Founders, it only provides for the ability to execute the powers already granted the federal government in the *Constitution*. But the problem is that, coupled with the new interpretations of the commerce clause, the feds have gotten their hands into almost everything."

"What should they be limited to?" Dave asked.

"In most of *Article 1, Section 8*, the Founders deliberately provided a list of the enumerated powers for the federal government. Had they intended to allow pretty much anything under the commerce clause and the necessary and proper clause they'd have been wasting their time enumerating the others.

"Is there any other evidence that the Founding Fathers actually meant to restrict the powers of the federal government?" I asked.

"Sure." He turned a page in the almanac. "In the *Preamble to the Bill of Rights* are included the words:

"The Conventions of a number of the States, having at the time of their adopting the *Constitution*, expressed a desire, in order to prevent misconstruction or abuse of its powers, that further declaratory and restrictive clauses should be added: And as extending the ground of

> ## Article V
>
> The Congress, whenever two thirds of both Houses shall deem it necessary, shall propose Amendments to this Constitution, or, on the Application of the Legislatures of two thirds of the several States, shall call a Convention for proposing Amendments, which, in either Case, shall be valid to all Intents and Purposes, as Part of this Constitution, when ratified by the Legislatures of three fourths of the several States, or by Conventions in three fourths thereof, as the one or the other Mode of Ratification may be proposed by the Congress; Provided that no Amendment which may be made prior to the Year One thousand eight hundred and eight shall in any Manner affect the first and fourth Clauses in the Ninth Section of the first Article; and that no State, without its Consent, shall be deprived of its equal Suffrage in the Senate.

public confidence in the Government, will best ensure the beneficent ends of its institution."

Mac continued, "The restrictive clauses added in the first ten Amendments are to restrict the federal government, not the states and, most assuredly, not the people."

"I didn't know there was a preamble," I said.

"It's usually omitted when the *Bill of Rights* is printed," Mac said. "But the wording in the Preamble is very important. It makes clear that those Amendments are there as further declaratory and restrictive clauses.

"But, despite the intention for a balance between the states and the feds, since the era of big government started in the 1930s, the federal government has pushed the envelope expanding and entrenching its powers and its pervasiveness in our society. This expansion has come at the expense of the rights of the people and the states. Of course, some people like it that way. Others have grumbled, but didn't know what to do about it. And the courts, which once held the federal government in check, also seem to have taken the attitude that bigger government is better government.

"However, lately, the feds have become ever more intrusive. Among the recent acts by the federal government that have finally triggered the

Tenth Amendment Movement is the pending Real ID Act, which amounts to a national identification system for all Americans. It was to go into effect in 2008 but because of resistance among the states, starting with Maine, the federal government has, temporarily, backed off on the Real ID Act. It is now due to take effect in 2011."

"What's wrong with the Real ID Act?" I asked.

"It creates a surveillance society. Remember when we were kids and we'd see movies about World War II Germany with Gestapo officers boarding trains or accosting people on the street and demanding to 'see their papers'? (We all knew what would happen if you didn't have your papers.) We recognized that as a sign of tyranny, and we used to say such an abuse of government authority could never happen here in the United States. Not in America, not in the land of the free!

"Well, it's here...or almost here, and freedom-loving Americans see it as one of the early steps to a society in which all citizens must be trackable by the federal government — or suffer penalties under the law.

"And there are more intrusions that are irking people. There's the whole Homeland Security thing; the No Child Left Behind Act, which is a federal intrusion into education; the National Animal Identification System, otherwise known as NAIS; land use laws; gun control; the Troubled Asset Relief Program, otherwise known as TARP, that the government has used lately to regulate the economy; and more.

"It's programs, rules, regulations, and laws, one after another, and they're in areas where many feel the federal government has clearly overstepped its bounds. So, after 70 years of federal high-handedness, the states are finally saying 'No!'"

Interpretation

"You say the increase in federal power has come about because of new interpretations of these clauses in the *Constitution*," I said. "What's the matter with reinterpreting it? Isn't that what makes it a living document?"

"It's living," Mac said with emphasis on the word 'living,' "only in that it can and should be amended by the rules set forth in *Article V* of the *Constitution*."

"You don't think we should be able to interpret the *Constitution* according to the needs of the times?" I asked.

He shook his head. "There is nothing in *Article V* that allows the *Constitution* to be changed or amended by interpretation. It was expected that changes to it would come from Congress or from a constitutional convention and that the states would have to approve them.

"Changes in the *Constitution* should be deliberated and decided by the people or their elected representatives, not a special interest, the Congress, or a President—both of whom the *Constitution* is supposed to protect us from—or some activist judge. Allowing them to change it through reinterpretation effectively flouts the Founders' intent."

"You could make the case that if the Founders wanted us to alter the *Constitution* with simple reinterpretation, they wouldn't have bothered including anything that's in *Article V*," Dave added.

"But how do we know what the *Constitution* is supposed to mean, anyway?" I asked. "Doesn't it always come down to who's interpreting it? Even as far as trying to figure out what the Founders meant?"

"No," Mac said. "The Founders left us all kinds of documents including letters and essays, among which are the Federalist Papers and the Anti-Federalist Papers, and they're pretty clear on what the wording of the *Constitution* means."

He got out of his seat again and went to Dave's computer and googled something on the Internet.

"For instance," he said when he apparently found what he was looking for, "as to the powers of the federal government, in number 45 of the Federalist Papers, James Madison, the man often referred to as 'The Father of the *Constitution*,' wrote:

"The powers delegated by the proposed *Constitution* to the federal government are few and defined.

"Keep that in mind: they're few and defined," he said, then continued reading:

"Those which are to remain in the State governments are numerous and indefinite. The former will be exercised principally on external objects, as war, peace, negotiation, and foreign commerce; with which last the power of taxation will, for the most part, be connected. The powers reserved to the several States will extend to all the objects which, in the ordinary course of affairs, concern the lives, liberties, and properties of the people, and the internal order, improvement, and prosperity of the State.

"Today, the courts, the Congress, Presidents, and the vast bureaucracy have turned the intent of those who framed the *Constitution*...our *Constitution*...on its head."

"What about a Constitutional Convention?" I asked. "I understand quite a few states have already called for one. Wouldn't that be the way to solve the problem? To write new Amendments that would restore the balance?"

"The last Constitutional Convention gave us the *Constitution* we now have," Mac said. "It's a pretty good one, if we just adhere to it. And today there's a new Convention being proposed. The call for it came about as a way to get a balanced budget amendment into the *Constitution* because it's not likely such an amendment will ever be proposed by Congress.

"So, let's say the call for a convention succeeds. Who's going to man it? Who are the delegates going to be? More specifically, where are the sort of people who gave us the *Constitution* we now have that's based on freedom and limited government? Where are the Jeffersons, Madisons, Masons, Franklins, and Washingtons who founded this country?"

Dave said, "I understand that one of the dangers of a

> ## Amendment IX
> The enumeration in the Constitution, of certain rights, shall not be construed to deny or disparage others retained by the people.

James Madison was one of the most important of the Founding Fathers. He is considered the "Father of the Constitution," of which he was the principal author, and he was one of the three men who wrote the Federalist Papers which are the best source of what the Founders intended when they wrote the Constitution. Madison also authored the Constitution's first ten Amendments, the Bill of Rights. He was an advocate of a government with checks and balances that would protect individual rights from the tyranny of the majority. He would go on to become the nation's fourth President.

Constitutional Convention is that, even if instructed by Congress, or even if a law were passed trying to put restraints on what the convention could consider, the members wouldn't be obligated to follow the orders and they could, in fact, rewrite the entire *Constitution*."

"That's true," Mac said. "If we have a second Constitutional Convention, we could see wholesale changes in the way this country is run and even major changes to the *Bill of Rights*. Do we want to risk that? A Constitutional Convention could be a catastrophe. Here's a partial list of things I think might change if today's politicians or their minions could rewrite the *Constitution*:

• Freedom of speech: We may get censorship through "hate crime" bills and the Fairness Doctrine.

• The right to trials: Prolonged detention without trial could become the norm.

• The right to bear arms: A repeal of the *Second Amendment* is a definite possibility.

• The right of assembly: We may be left only with the right to free speech zones.

• Property rights: Kiss those goodbye because they will become collective rights and seizure laws, which are truly unconstitutional, may become codified.

"Furthermore, the hallmark of the rights the Founders claimed we have is that they didn't have to be provided, with the notable exception to the right to a jury trial. But if the *Bill of Rights* were rewritten, expect rights to be included such as a right to healthcare, a job, an income, etc. Unlike the Natural or God-given rights that we all have naturally, these man-made rights will have to be man-provided, too, and they will have to be paid for and provided by you and me.

"The only safeguard we would have is that any and all changes a constitutional convention might bring would still have to be approved by three quarters of the states. But who would want to let it get that far?

"The amendment process should never be taken lightly and, in today's political climate, a constitutional convention should not be considered at all."

"Give me the bottom line," Dave said. "What would it mean if the Tenth Amendment Movement succeeded?"

"The federal government will have to start behaving by the terms of *Article I, Section 8*, the *Ninth Amendment*, and the *Tenth Amendment*. It will mean more decisions can and will be made locally regarding education, land use, etc. It'll also lead to more individual freedoms. It will most likely mean an end to the idea of a surveillance society."

Who's for it? Who's against it?

"Who wants it and who's against the Tenth Amendment Movement?" I asked.

"It's significant that at least three dozen states have introduced it into their legislatures. So it can't be characterized as a fringe movement. But if it picks up even more steam, you can expect that to be one of the accusations made against it.

"It's also been promoted or opposed along party lines. When the resolution has been introduced into the various state legislatures, the yea votes have been largely Republican and Libertarian while those who oppose reestablishing the balance of power between the states and the federal government have been Democrats. Mind you, the Republicans are not solidly behind it, nor are the Democrats solidly against it, but that's pretty much how the votes have gone. Libertarians are solidly behind it."

"So, who else opposes it?" Dave asked.

"The irony is that the very people we send to Congress — our representatives and senators — are likely to oppose it."

"That makes sense," Dave said. "They're the manufacturers of big government. They're the ones who want the new spin put on the commerce clause."

Mac nodded.

"Members of America's mammoth bureaucracy will also oppose it," Mac said.

"Their jobs depend on big government," Dave interjected and Mac nodded again.

"And there are many people in this country who want a strong central government. It wouldn't surprise me if many wouldn't balk at the institution of a dictatorship — if it could be the dictatorship of their choosing.

"And a lot of people will buy into the accusation that the Tenth Amendment Movement is just a mask for a secessionist movement, so they'll oppose it not so much out of self-interest as ignorance. New Hampshire's resolution was characterized as such by its opponents, so it lost when it was introduced to the legislature. But it's likely to be reintroduced."

"How do you think the movement is going to fare?" Dave asked.

Mac smiled ruefully and said, "I'm cautiously optimistic, which is another way of saying I hope it succeeds but I don't have much hope for it. And for quite a few reasons."

"Like what?" I asked.

"When it comes down to the reasons why they are intruding in our lives, the government argues that it's the only way it can function efficiently. The logical counterargument is that by doing so, the government infringes on our rights. But the concept of rights is becoming more and more abstract for the average voter."

"Furthermore, the average voter doesn't even know what's in the *Constitution*, never mind what *Article I, Section 8*, the *Ninth Amendment*, or the *Tenth Amendment* say.

"Then there's past history and the way the public behaves."

"What do you mean?" I asked.

"In 1994 Americans threw both houses of Congress to the Republicans on the basis of the promises they made in their Contract with America to rein in big government. But once they had power, with the exception of some of their freshman senators and representatives, the Republican Party turned its back on most of its own 'contract' and the federal government continued with business as usual. And what did the voters do? They did what they always do. They reelected them.

"What kind of message does that send to politicians about not keeping their promises?"

Dave said, "If you think about it, Mac, we already have the way to bring about change at our disposal, and we can do it without a Tenth Amendment Movement, without a constitutional amendment, and without a constitutional convention."

Mac nodded. He knew.

"What is it?" I asked.

"If we really want to see power returned to the states, all we have to do is vote almost all of the guys currently in office out. It's the very men and women We the People are sending to Congress who are leading the charge to empower the federal government even more. If we throw them out, and keep throwing them out when they trample on our rights, we can have the kind of government we're supposed to have."

"And because of these things, I'm not too optimistic about the movement's future," Mac said.

"But," he said as he rose from his seat again, "I am optimistic about fishing the Rogue this morning. So, I'm out of here."

"Wanna go?" Dave asked me.

"Sure," I replied. And with that, all three of us went out the door. Δ

Other titles available from
Backwoods Home Magazine

The Best of the First Two Years
A Backwoods Home Anthology—The Third Year
A Backwoods Home Anthology—The Fourth Year
A Backwoods Home Anthology—The Fifth Year
A Backwoods Home Anthology—The Sixth Year
A Backwoods Home Anthology—The Seventh Year
A Backwoods Home Anthology—The Eighth Year
A Backwoods Home Anthology—The Ninth Year
A Backwoods Home Anthology—The Tenth Year
A Backwoods Home Anthology—The Eleventh Year
A Backwoods Home Anthology—The Twelfth Year
A Backwoods Home Anthology—The Thirteenth Year
A Backwoods Home Anthology—The Fourteenth Year
Emergency Preparedness and Survival Guide
Backwoods Home Cooking
Can America Be Saved From Stupid People
Chickens—a beginner's handbook
Starting Over—Chronicles of a Self-Reliant Woman
Dairy Goats—a beginner's handbook
Self-reliance—Recession-proof your pantry
Making a Living—Creating your own job
Harvesting the Wild—gathering & using food from nature
Growing and Canning Your Own Food